WHO'S LAUGHING NOW ?

Feminist Perspectives on Humour and Laughter

Edited by Anna Frey

DEMETER

Who's Laughing Now?

Feminist Perspectives on Humour and Laughter

Edited by Anna Frey

Copyright © 2021 Demeter Press

Demeter Press
2546 10th Line
Bradford, Ontario
Canada, L3Z 3L3
Tel: 289-383-0134
Email: info@demeterpress.org
Website: www.demeterpress.org

Demeter Press logo based on the sculpture "Demeter" by Maria-Luise Bodirsky www.keramik-atelier.bodirsky.de

Printed and Bound in Canada

Cover artwork: Denise Audette
Typesetting: Michelle Pirovich

Library and Archives Canada Cataloguing in Publication
Title: Who's laughing now?: feminist perspectives on humour and laughter / edited by Anna Frey.
Names: Frey, Anna 1991- editor.
Description: Includes bibliographical references.
Identifiers: Canadiana 2020037415X | ISBN 9781772582833 (softcover)
Subjects: LCSH: Feminism—Humor. | LCSH: Feminists—Humor. | LCSH: Women—Humor.
Classification: LCC HQ1233.W46 2021 | DDC 305.42—dc23

Acknowledgments

First of all, there would be no book without the commitment and generosity of each and every contributor included within. Thank you for your patience through endless emails, deadline reminders, and last-minute edits. A huge thank you as well to the invisible-to-me team of people who prop each of you up: your friends, families, and supportive coworkers. Let them celebrate you!

The reliable cheerleading from my spouse, Max Morin, and the ever-more gentle inquiries from my mother, Sandra Petersen-Frey, buoyed my confidence during the tougher moments of writing my own contribution. I am grateful to May Friedman for suggesting I pitch this collection to Demeter Press and for her expert insight into how this whole publishing thing works.

I am indebted to the peer reviewers, who took the time to read these chapters thoughtfully. Your energy and edits made this book stronger. The team at Demeter Press had faith in this collection from the get-go, despite it being an unconventional topic on their roster—thank you! Denise Audette, who designed the gorgeous cover, engaged me in a generative creative process, and I feel richer for it.

To those who shared the initial call for submissions through their networks, pitched ideas that weren't able to be included, preordered copies, or generally hyped up the collection at any time, you have the appreciation of everyone included here. May we one day have the chance to meet and share some laughs together.

Contents

Introduction

Anna Frey

I hear women laughing. I hear them at family reunions, my grandmother hooting with my aunts, my mother laughing to herself at the rest of us. I hear them where I work as a sexual health counsellor on the phone, women chuckling over the line at the situations they have found themselves in. And in my role as an abortion counsellor, I sometimes hear women apologizing to me for laughing, as though they were the only ones who laugh, as though they could somehow offend me. I hear women laughing, and I am again and again reminded of our extraordinary capacity for flexibility and resilience.

Laughter comes from the body, and women's bodies live within contexts of misogyny, transphobia, racism, violence, privilege, and pleasure. A feminist approach to laughter is conscious of humour's rhetorical power: Jokes can guide us towards curiosity, provoke moments of insight and critical thought, and help us to build bridges between our communities and allies. Of course, not all women practice feminism, and women's comedy can just as much reinforce violent systems of oppression as refute them. This book attempts to untangle some of the complicated snarls feminist laughers of all genders find ourselves in. In what ways is feminist humour succeeding, and how do we measure that success? What is at stake in the struggle over whether or not women can be funny? What resources do we need in place to support those of us who perform feminist comedy and are targets of harassment and trolling? How are politics communicated through jokes and memes, and how can we develop media literacy skills to both critique and create funny content? Although the exact focus of these questions changes with the sociopolitical and media landscapes of the time, discussions about humour's place within feminist movements have been happening for decades.

Feminist activists have long recognized and taken up laughter as political action and a mechanism of self-care. In her 1994 interview with

Judith Butler, Rosi Braidotti speaks of the "subversive force of Dionysian laughter" and invites modern feminists to partake more liberally in these joyful disruptions (41). Feminists have recognized laughter's range of applications, from the merrymaking Braidotti desires, to how Annie Leclerc imagines laughter having the power of a weapon to pierce and deflate patriarchal values, and to Hélène Cixous's claim in her "Laugh of the Medusa" that women's laughter is erotic and generative (Parvulescu 112; Cixous). Despite this work, accusations of humourlessness have been levied at feminists for years. Of course, it is worth remembering who spouts these accusations and which kinds of humour they are defending. Proponents of misogynist jokes are quick to lambast feminists for our complaints about that content, but then they issue threats to silence us once we start telling jokes about the men who have caused us harm. The message is clear: Feminists and feminism are to be the butt and nothing but. This insistence on silencing our laughter belies how menacing it can be. Defiant humour and laughter are dangers to the dominant order because, as Cris Mayo suggests, they can "affect the stability of meaning and the structure of political power" with their disruptive potential (513).

Attributions of humourlessness come from within feminism as well as from without. We are still posing questions to each other about whether it is possible (or beneficial) to have a feminism that incorporates wit, sarcasm, or buffoonery, and if we accept laughter as part of our movement, what topics, if any, are off limits? Although the authors included in this collection all agree that joyous, ribald, and sometimes spiteful laughter have their place within feminism, they embrace the dynamic nature of these conversations and add their voices to the mix not in an attempt to have the final word on the matter but to contribute new perspectives to hopefully long-lasting discussions. The chapters that follow are aligned with the delightful, disorderly irony Sara Ahmed has embraced by labelling herself a Feminist Killjoy—simultaneously performing an in-group wink, a smirk, and a steady gaze held until the other backs down.

In the opening chapter, "I Would Come Up With a Funny Title, but I'm Just a Girl: Women, Comedy, and an Evolved Sense of Humour," Vanessa Voss tackles the big question of the gender divide in humour. Using evolutionary biology, she counters the sexist assertion that women just do not have the right brain for comedy; instead, she asserts that the capacity for recognizing and creating humour is a fundamental human process that has played a key role in our evolution and survival as a species. Voss organizes these arguments around critical engagements with the production of the animated television series *Rick and Morty* and the internet cartoon *Cyanide and Happiness*. Using these texts, she both shows and tells us that, despite what misogynist trolls on *Reddit* may have to say, the disadvantages women in comedy face are generated culturally, not biologically, and are steadily shrinking through the power of feminist pushbacks.

Natalja Chestopalova picks up the thread of femme feminist pushbacks in chapter two, "Phenomenology Of a Feminist Joke and the Quintessential Emotional Labour in Maria Bamford's Comedy." She frames humour as a dialogue rich with possibilities for critical growth: "A good feminist joke that incites laughter is nothing less than a confession that there are still questions to be formulated about what narratives are prevalent, what voices are absent, what issues remain taboos, and what kinds of activist emotional labour remain vital." Bamford tackles the twin issues of emotional labour and self-care on screen as she pulls back the veil on the ableism, racism, sexism, and ageism she has encountered within the entertainment industry. Chestopalova uses a phenomenological approach to bring us closer to the heart of what consuming feminist comedy can teach us as well as the implications it can have towards challenging patriarchal culture.

These threads of emotional labour and systemic oppression weave through chapter three, "I Have To Laugh, or I'll Die," where Toronto-based stand-up comic Aba Amuquandoh offers us her personal reflections on growing up and coming to see comedy as a route towards solace. Her experiences of loss and grief, alienation through racism, and coming out to herself and her friend inform her approach to writing and performing live humour. This chapter demonstrates how the theories different authors work with in this collection play out in the real lives of working comics.

My own contribution to this collection, "'Man, That Guy's Sad... but He *Killed*': Survivors Of Sexual Violence Joke about Rape," grew from a yearning to see reactions to rape culture that hit affective notes other than rage and sorrow. This chapter features interviews I did with stand-up comics who perform material about being survivors of sexual violence. These participants pushed back on the cultural assumption that survivors ought to remain weepy and chastened when discussing the violence they had endured. By supporting their testimonies with critical feminist and trauma theories I argue that stand-up comedy has the potential to be a source of healing and community building for people living with sexual trauma.

In chapter five, "The *Bad Mothers Club*: In Cyberspace You Can Hear the Unruly Women Laughing," Anitra Goriss-Hunter guides us towards motherhood's worst-kept secret: the *Bad Mothers Club*. This website is a refuge for mothers who feel they do not cohere to Western society's expectations of good mothering. Goriss-Hunter pulls examples from this living feminist text that demonstrates mothers' need to poke fun at the children, spouses, social pressures, and other mothers who dominate their lives. The *Bad Mothers Club*, as she describes it, is a place to find community and blow off steam, but it is not a feminist utopia. Despite the razor-sharp humour that moderators and commenters often employ, material posted on the site can sometimes be seen to hold up the same traditional values it seeks to tear down. Goriss-Hunter picks at the complicated knot this presents and fleshes out the multifaceted ways in which mothers share their own experiences online.

In chapter six, "Making It Up As They Go Along: An Analysis of Feminist Comedy in the Prairies," Marley Duckett keeps us locked in on the experience of generating feminist comedy by bringing us to Saskatoon, Saskatchewan, home of LadyBits Improv Comedy Collective. Duckett takes us through the history of live comedy in the Prairies to the present day, where LadyBits, founded by herself and two colleagues, offers an alternative to the otherwise male-dominated comedy scene. She is generous and lively in her storytelling, and her reflections on the opposition, growing pains, and successes LadyBits has weathered offer a valuable roadmap for other comedy practitioners looking to shake up their local scenes.

Sai Amulya Komarraju's chapter, "'Immoral, Slut, Arsehole': Feminist Memes Reclaim Stereotypes," encourages more questions about doing feminism in the network. Who has access to these online spaces? How can feminist activists use the internet to expose more people to their messages? What is the relationship between online and offline practices of resistance? Through her analysis of the meme campaign The Spoilt Modern Indian Woman, Komarraju offers us tributaries towards a richer understanding of the above questions and the sociopolitical contexts in which feminist activists are working in India today. She draws from a number of examples of memes the campaign has promoted, and she argues that their humour and their crowd-sourced nature are crucial in generating ongoing interest and participation in this type of virtual resistance.

In chapter eight, "Queens Of the Castle: Intergenerational Conversations about Elaine Benes's (Imperfect) Feminism," Stephanie Patrick and Hayley R. Crooks conduct a methodologically refreshing investigation into the character of Elaine Benes from *Seinfeld*. They use autoethnographies alongside interviews with their own mothers to locate Elaine's potential as a cross-generational feminist bridge. During the interviews and analysis, they locate *Seinfeld* within its context of production and compare their mothers' reactions to other women-led sitcoms, such as *Roseanne* and the *Mary Tyler Moore Show*. By looking at Elaine's reception by women over time and across social circumstances, Crooks and Patrick present us with a nuanced interpretation of funny feminist characters on the small screen and the multigenerational impacts they can have.

How do different social groups respond when faced with mean-spirited jokes and accusations of humourlessness? In chapter nine, "Lighten Up!: Life as a Vegetarian Feminist, or the Most Uptight Person in the World," Margaret Betz draws on her own identifications as a feminist and as a vegetarian to explore the similarities and differences between how American society treats each of these groups and how they, in turn, respond. Her analysis is a bookend to some of the questions Voss raises in chapter one. Readers are treated once more to a feminist confrontation with Christopher Hitchens's insistent misogyny. Although feminism has a colourful history of responding to oppression with humour, Betz raises the point that the vegetarian movement has not yet embraced these rhetorical tactics. The work she accomplishes here reminds us of the radical possibilities of approaching issues of bodily autonomy and environmentalism, among others, with confident laughter.

In the final chapter, "That Time I Tried to Date a Frat Boy," Alyson Rogers delights and disgusts with tales from her attempt to date a frat boy and reform his wayward brothers. From sanitizing the frat house to offering impromptu workshops on consent between songs at the bar, Rogers puts her social work degree to good use and volunteers all of the grimy details. Pay attention to Rogers's turns of phrase, callbacks, and insider jokes. This creative piece gives us the opportunity to practice taking humour seriously, and the study and reflection prompts included at the end of it are just a launching point.

Closing the book with a lighthearted piece of comedy gives us more than one more text for analysis—it also gives us a moment of relief. Feminism is a serious, often life-or-death movement towards bodily autonomy for all. But, like any movement, it is made up of individual people who need relief, who need to play, and who need their humanity recognized. Laughter is one tool to help us in this struggle—and scholar-practitioners like Amuquandoh, Duckett, and Rogers remind that laughter is feminist praxis.

The title of this book, the question "who's laughing now?"—is a call towards reflection, regardless of how defiant it sounds. Who is laughing? And why? Feminist laughter can be wild, triumphant, bitter, glib, fearful, erotic, emancipatory, and on and on. There are endless reasons to laugh as well as to abstain from laughter. We must treat feminist laughter not as an obligation but as an opportunity to exercise the full freedom we have over our bodies and our voices.

Works Cited

Braidotti, Rosi, and Judith Butler. "Feminism by Any Other Name." *Differences: A Journal of Feminist Cultural Studies*, vol. 6, no. 2, 1994, pp. 27-61.

Cixous, Hélène. "Laugh of the Medusa." *New French Feminisms: An Anthology*, edited by Elaine Marks and Isabelle de Courtivron, University of Massachusetts Press, 1980, pp. 245-64.

Mayo, Cris. "Incongruity and Provisional Safety: Thinking through Humour." *Studies in Philosophy and Education*, vol. 29, no. 6, 2010, pp. 509-21.

Parvulescu, Anca. *Laughter: Notes on a Passion*. MIT Press, 2010.

Chapter One

I Would Come Up with a Funny Title, but I'm Just a Girl: Women, Comedy, and an Evolved Sense of Humour

Vanessa Voss

Introduction

In season three of the animated television show *Rick and Morty*, female writers were brought in to balance the gender gap in the writing room. Many male fans attacked the female writers. The women received threats of violence on *Twitter* and had their personal information made public online, a practice called "doxing." Fans of *Rick and Morty* took to *Reddit* to verbally condemn the show. Threads of *Rick and Morty* discussion boards complained about how the show now glorified gynocentrism and had become another platform for the social justice warrior (SJW) culture, just like *South Park*.[1] Fans complained that now that women were writers on the show, the show focused more on family dynamics and the female characters; thus, the so-called smart humour had been lost due to that feminine touch. A handful of fans suggested revenge on the writers by not paying to watch the show, but instead pirating it through illegal viewing sites, such as *Pirate Bay* or *Putlocker*. If the show did not get any revenue from the show, it would die, and the writers would suffer. "Fuck them. I hope they starve to death. I will steal the nails off of their studio walls if I have to," as one *Reddit* thread commenter railed (nopussy_ona_pedestal, Reddit thread). The *Reddit* users complained of the women being hired as "quota women" and only to fill a gender gap as demanded by a women-centered society. Although some commenters argued that *Rick and Morty* had not been ruined and that women were funny, most *Reddit* threads were misogynistic and aggressive in tone. Their justification for their hostile behaviour was that women did not belong in this writing room and that women did not (and could not) understand the humour of the show (Saraiya). Women would ruin *Rick and Morty* not only because it is not a show with "women's humour" but also because women generally lack a sense of humour, at least in comparison to men. *Rick and Morty* is about the antics of a mad scientist travelling in infinite universes: it is, therefore, too scientific for women to understand and, thus, write jokes for. And women just are not funny anyways.[2]

The show's creators, Dan Harmon and Justin Roiland, defended their new writers and lamented the backlash. In an interview, Harmon said, "The day there is a female writer in that writer's room, that person is definitely not going to be thinking that they're a quota writer" (qtd. in Gajewski). Roiland added that those in the writing room were there based on their own merit.[3] Harmon also pointed to the fact that there are no shows written exclusively by just one person, so the fans had failed to understand the creation process in television writing and production. All episodes are a group production: if you hate the show, you hate the whole crew, not just a few women writers.[4]

This incident is just one of many in a long history of the idea that women are not funny. There is a long tradition of harassment directed towards women being funny and at those who would dare support these funny women. How should we respond to the claim that women lack humour in both comprehending and creating it? In this chapter, I am going to give a brief sketch of the history of the claim that women are not funny, ultimately focusing on Christopher Hitchens's *Vanity Fair* article, "Why Women Aren't Funny" (2007). I will then refute Hitchens's idea, put forth either as a joke or in earnest, that evolution has shaped women's biology in such a way as to condemn them to boorishness. Coming to the aid of gender-parity in the evolution of humour is Matthew Hurley, Daniel Dennett, and Reginald Adams's book *Inside Jokes: Using Humour to Reverse-Engineer the Mind* (2011). The conclusion I draw from their research is that if women do not appear funny, biology is not to blame; rather, the culprit is the long history of misogyny and the oppression of women's humorous voices.

What? Women Aren't Funny? A Brief History

As Gabrielle Moss has said, "As long as there have been jokes, there have been people saying that women can't tell them." In Genesis, Sarah laughed to herself when God, through a messenger, said she should bear a child in her old age. But of course, the joke is told by God, and she is laughing to herself. The joke is heralded by a male. In more recent history, many male comedians have made it clear that they believe men to be funnier than women, and, even if women are funny, there are by far more funny men than women. On *Saturday Night Live*, John Belushi repeatedly requested that the women writers on staff be fired.[5] Adam Carrolla said, "The reason why you know more funny dudes than funny chicks is that dudes are funnier than chicks" (qtd. in Moss). However, these men are not saying or doing anything new.

In 1695, in an essay on humour, playwright William Congreve wrote that women's passions are "too powerful," thus impeding any chance of being funny. Humour requires coolness and detachment, and women's nature is the opposite. Richard Grant White, a cultural critic in the 1800s, wrote that humour in a woman was the rarest of qualities (Moss). The "humourlessness of women" was a common theme in magazines, such as *Punch* in the early 1900s (Stanley).[6] In 2000, Jerry Lewis told an audience that he just did not like any female comedians. Another male comedian on stage at the time, Martin Short, asked Lewis what he thought about (allegedly) funny woman Lucille Ball. Apparently, in the end, Lewis did not love Lucy (Stanley). And let us not forget the *Ghostbusters* (2016) revival, in which wise-cracking women would save New York once more from the supernatural. Male online trolls clamoured that the women (Melissa McCarthy, Kristen Wiig, Kate McKinnon, and Leslie Jones) were not funny, and thus not fit, to wear the same jumpsuits as stars like Bill Murray and Dan Ackroyd.

One must acknowledge that there is research pointing to the fact that men routinely make more jokes and attempts at humour than women. In a 2011 study, evolutionary psychologist Gil Greengross found that men make jokes more often, or at least "joke attempts." In this data, there lies evidence for the assumption that, since men make more jokes (or attempts), they must be funnier (even when they are not). The study shows, however, that although men do make more jokes, but many are failed attempts. Neuroscientist and professor of psychology Robert Provine, in his book *Laughter: A Scientific Investigation* (2000), argues that women do laugh more in response to men's jokes than women's jokes while making fewer jokes themselves. Women are also less likely to make jokes in dialogue with men; although they do joke more with other women, they refrain more often in the presence of men (Provine 27-35). Men routinely rank themselves as funnier than women, and women routinely rank men as funnier than they are (Kazan). This research also points to another trend in heterosexual relationships: Men want women who will laugh at their jokes (but not at them, of course), and women tend to romantically want men who make them laugh. But let us not forget: Women do laugh and joke with each other when men are not around.[7]

Let us now turn to the infamous 2007 *Vanity Fair* article by Christopher Hitchens fittingly titled "Why Women Aren't Funny." In this article, Hitchens argues that biological evolution is the basis for women being less funny than men are. He argues that women have no need to appeal to men through humour, so they have not evolved the same "funny bone" as men. Men, in contrast, need humour to seduce women. Thus, when men have a big, throbbing funny bone, women cannot help but become aroused and sexually interested (and readily available). He acknowledges that women can be funny, but he claims for men, it occurs more naturally.

Women's role in reproductive success is a more serious role, Hitchens says, and this leaves the average woman as humourless as a suffragette. Giving birth is the higher calling for women, but it is also a higher calling that makes them the boss in the biological world. Women pick and choose with whom they will reproduce; they decide the fate of reproduction. Men make jokes to put women into a state of mirth to attract them, so men have to do the work of attraction in order to please their boss. Women, as the boss, decide who they will hire and who they will fire sexually, and this is a serious business for the fate of the species. Women cannot afford much frivolity and play in the way that men can, Hitchens says, in light of their important role in reproduction. It is a solemn responsibility and grave work, both physically and emotionally, to give birth and to raise a child—to continue the species. It is life or death. To use Hitchens's example comparing the seriousness of women's work in comparison to men's, he says women are the bearers of religion, of the sacred, while men are the bearers of the obscene, the dirty joke: "For men, it is a tragedy that the two things they prize the most—women and humour—should be so antithetical."[8]

Many articles replied to Hitchens's claim, arguing that it is not a biological fact that women are not funny; rather, society moulds women to shun their funny bone and to focus more on being physically attractive to men. In response to Hitchens, Alessandra Stanley wrote, "Society has different expectations for women ... the rewards of wit are not nearly as ample for women as for men, and sometimes funny women are actually penalized."[9] Hitchens replied in a 2008 article that he was still correct in his views and that those who criticized him, like Stanley, only proved his point that evolution has made men funnier than women. In his article, he writes that Stanley agrees with him that women have no imperative to be funny in the same way that men do. He takes Stanley's direct words and claims she is saying the exact same thing that he is saying, missing her main point that it is more of a cultural construct than a product of biological imperatives. In the article, it seems he is too busy trying to flirt via *Vanity Fair* with the "tawny Alessandra" who "pads so lovingly in the deep tracks" of his argument on why women are not funny. Stanley agrees with me, although she hides it, Hitchens seems to say; according to Hitchens, she hides it because she may be aroused by him.[10]

Maybe funny woman Joan Rivers was right: "Women should look good. Work on yourselves. Education? I spit on education. No man is ever going to put his hand up your dress looking for a library card" (qtd. in Dockterman). Maybe our biology is our destiny, and it just is not a funny one. However, Hitchens fails to recognize the crucial point: The operative selective evolutionary mechanism is cultural, not biological.

A Real Evolutionary Response: Hurley, Dennett, and Adams Walk into an Argument

By giving an evolutionary explanation of humour itself, it is easy to show that Hitchens is clearly wrong in his biology-based claim that man evolved to be funnier than woman. Women must have the cognitive function of humour and mirth, just as they must have other evolved cognitive functions, such as memory and pattern recognition. If Hurley, Dennett, and Adams are correct, what humour does in the brain, in creating it and responding to it, is essential to the survival of all humans. They argue that humour is a necessary mental operation, necessary for cleaning up bad inferences. Men and women both require this mental operation, this cleaning, for the wellbeing of thinking. If men are perceived as funnier, a purely biological evolutionary explanation fails to explain it.

The overarching purpose that drives the brain is survival; thus the brain is hardwired to achieve that purpose as best as it can, given a myriad of limitations. How does it do this job so well? It anticipates and predicates, in real time, possible changes to environment. The brain must also attend to the appropriate things—those things necessary to attend to for survival and not the millions of other possible things it could be attending to (Hurley et al. 95). It is with this survival need of anticipation and attention that Hurley, Dennett, and Adams begin their explanation of what is known as the Hurley model of humour.

Evolution addresses the survival needs of anticipation and attention by the "on-demand creation of mental spaces" (Hurley et al. 98). These are creative spaces in which thought can maintain different referents at one time. The "on-demand creation of mental spaces "may be compared to having different browser tabs open at the same time on your laptop, just in case one is suddenly needed, perhaps even unexpectedly. (You never know when you'll need to engage with corgiorgy.com, so you better keep that tab open.) The tabs are all open at the same time, but they each constitute a separate space. We humans are constantly making predictions about the meaning of events, words, and ideas that seem hazy and uncertain. Thus, we are always readjusting our mental space, and reopening and closing our mental tabs. This readjusting happens as new information enters our mental space, so this readjustment is always happening. New information enters constantly, and our mental spaces search again for the right prediction or meaning (finding the tabs to attend to), then they readjust, reorient, search, and repeat. This is the work of the human mind—a constant process of (re)framing.[11]

But not all anticipations and predictions come to pass. We, as humans, expect future events to fall in line with our experiences, but there are many more possibilities that could occur. We attempt to form appropriate expectations but often fail to because we cannot attend to that many tabs. Given our reservoir of experiences, we have good reason to expect a certain chain of events, but it simply may not occur. An example will help make this clearer.

Here is a scene with reasonable expectations and predictions. A man at a restaurant orders soup. He looks in the soup and sees a variety of letters in the noodles. A waiter comes up to the man and asks, "How is your alphabet soup?" The man replies, "A little salty but good." We have experienced interactions similar to this many times, at home and in restaurants. We could easily predict what events were going to happen and mentally be ready for them. It is easy to predict this in our creative mental spaces. This is just a regular, reasonable, and pedestrian event. However, a cartoon from *Cyanide and Happiness* takes us in a different direction.[12]

Would our fast-action, frame-generator brain correctly predict this scenario? (Fig. 1. DenBleyker, *Cyanide and Happiness*).

Cyanide and Happiness © Explosm.net

Why do we find this humorous? Hurley, Dennett, and Adams argue it is because an assumption has been "epistemically committed to in a mental space" but now has been "discovered to be a mistake" (Hurley et al. 121). We are given a restaurant scene and could not have predicted what happened. (This might have been a Google tab a million places to the right of the browser.) We committed to a particular chain of events as probable, but we were in error. But, thankfully, this error in commitment was not fatal or detrimental to our survival. Everything is okay. This is where the reward of mirth can be found.

Drawing on research in the creation of mental spaces, beliefs, and anticipation, the Hurley model of humour claims that mirth (the psychological associate of humour) occurs when five things happen in an experience:

1. An active element in a mental space has

2. Covertly entered that space ... and is

3. Taken to be true (i.e. epistemically committed) with that space

4. Is diagnosed to be false in that space—simply in the sense that it is the loser in the epistemic reconciliation process;

5. And (trivially) the discovery is not accompanied by any (strong) negative emotional valance. (Hurley et al. 121)

We can apply this to the preceding comic. The joke's setup primes a set of assumptions based on our experiences at restaurants. These assumptions or expectations frame the narrative for us and are implicitly taken to be true—but then they turn out to be false. Thus, the pleasurable dining experience and innocence of the soup are called into question, as is the usual meaning of salty in this setting. But we are not harmed by this erroneous framing of the situation as it shifts. Nothing is going to maul us for mistaking a restaurant scene's events, unlike mistaking a tiger for a colourful rock. We will be rewarded in the discovery of this nonthreatening error in the form of mirth. Hurley, Dennett, and Adams argue that mirth is a special reward, a "one-to-one mapping between the qualia of reward and the distinctive triggering circumstance to identify it," given for a very distinct "cognitive circumstance" that is distinctly human: mirth, "the discovery of an overcommitment to a covertly held belief" (124).[13] We are rewarded with mirth only when the epistemic commitment is shown to be false but also benign.

But this experience should feel negative, right? Our model of the world has let us down—we assumed a frame was false, even if not disastrously false. Why are we rewarded with mirth by our brains when our brains went wrong? On the Hurley model of humour, a humorous event does point to an error in reasoning or knowledge that leads to a false belief in both individuals and observers of individuals. This error of reasoning or knowledge can give us a sense of surprise in our error, but this data breach is immediately corrected within the joke. When we read the comic, we are initially surprised but then immediately realize that in this particular situation, "salty" means "sassy," and not high sodium content, as is usually the case in restaurant dialogue.

In this case, mirth has an adaptive function: "to encourage a particular task of knowledge maintenance" (Hurley et al. 289). We are rewarded with mirth when we recognize our framing errors so that we are encouraged to keep our mind informationally up to date. This vital clean-up job is rewarded with mirth. Just as other tasks vital to survival are rewarded with pleasure—for example, high-caloric intake is rewarded with the taste of sweetness (a mechanism evolved in an environment of caloric scarcity) and mating is rewarded with sexual pleasure—mirth rewards our mind for cleaning up bad inferences.[14]

The Hurley model of humour, as briefly outlined here, claims that all humans have a "very specific error elimination capacity," which ends in our experience of mirth (Hurley et al. 12). In our mental space, we generate presumptions about what will happen, and this list of possibilities is open as content in our mental space. Not all of this content can be fact checked in time, so many of our predictions and inferences are left unexamined.[15] Errors, thus, occur, and nonfatal or benign errors, when resolved and shown to be such, will arouse the feeling of mirth to reward our discovery of the error and its correction. And this is for all humans (Hurley et al. 12-13).

With this evolutionary explanation under our belts and bras, we can return with new insights to our primary concern in this paper: the claim that men are funnier than women for biological-evolutionary reasons. Although it may be that men make more jokes than women and are perceived as being funnier than women, on the Hurley model of humour, it seems this proposed thesis is not a product of our evolved biology. Evolution has not made this the case; these biological facts of women not being funny are more likely gender qualities that have evolved culturally. Humour, especially told between people in the form of jokes, bears the mark of cultural communication and "evolves into a medium for the display of intelligence and mutual knowledge and opinion" (Hurley et al. 291). Jokes are an artifact intentionally created by humans as super-normal stimuli (much like candy is an artifact for sweet and pornography is an artifact for sexual pleasure).[16]

A sense of humour as being a predominately masculine trait has arisen from social evolution; it is not an innate biological difference between men and women. Hurley, Dennett, and Adams write that "[A] debugging mechanism that serves epistemic purposes will be equally useful for both genders" (295). They point to why males are perceived as funnier than females: the pursuit of sexual attention from females.[17] This is the point that Hitchens wants to argue for in his essay. But if humour has a cultural history as "reinforced behavioural prospecting" of catching female attention, then that idea, that meme, will be used, reused, and promoted through cultural reinforcement. It is not, as Hitchens claims, that biology created men to be funnier than women but that we have culturally reinforced the idea that funny men win women and that women want funny men. The unfunny female will, thus, also be culturally promoted as a win for women.

Hurley, Dennett, and Adams point to the presentation of humour as a show of intelligence, saying that "telling someone a joke is as much flattery as it is showing off ... [it is] the medium for the display of intelligence and mutual knowledge" (291). Jokes show a kind of wit and intelligence and emerge in a cultural ecosystem all of their own.

For example, let's consider a particular internet humour page: "Nihilist Arby's" on *Twitter* (Fig. 2 @nihilist_arbys *Nihilist Arby's*. 20 Jan 2015).

Nihilist Arby's @nihilist_arbys   20 Jan 2015
There's no god so why not worship our smokehouse brisket? You'll literally get the same results.

⤺   ♻ 407   ♥ 536   •••

To create jokes on the meaninglessness of existence, one must have a certain set of knowledge on the subject of the absurd and of the core beliefs of nihilism. And to create a successful meme, the creator must structure that content well to express the joke, which requires an understanding of how jokes are best expressed between people or how memes are often expressed. To understand these jokes, a viewer or listener must know something about the content in them as well.

Otherwise, the joke will be lost on the viewer or listener. To follow this Nihilist Arby's joke, the teller must understand at least a simple historical knowledge of how Arby's is perceived, what nihilism entails, and what format, length, and language that content should take to be perceived as funny. The listener must also need to have a basic level of understanding of these as well to understand the joke and to laugh at it. And recall Provine's research: Women do laugh more than men, and laughter does entail knowing what the joke is about. Women do get it.

When women are believed to not be as funny as men, hidden in that claim is also the belief that women are not as intelligent as men. Recall that one of the concerns about having female writers on *Rick and Morty* was that women could not really understand the humour on the show and would not understand the intellectual content. It is easy to draw a parallel between the history of "women are not as funny as men" to the history of "women are not as rational as men" or "women are not as intelligent as men."[18] Claims of the superiority of male intelligence over female are dubious and do not hold under scientific scrutiny. Although male and females may have some differences in their brain structures, the effects of this difference on overall intelligence is unclear. It does seem clear that women have evolved the same cognitive faculties as men that are needed for basic survival; great differences in intelligence, therefore, seem unlikely, as a certain level of intelligence may be necessary for sexual reproduction and survival for all humans. Clearly, women get it. They laugh and, on average, more than men. They may tell fewer jokes, but that does not make them humourless. Humour is not a biologically determined trait.

Women have the same intellectual capabilities as men when they are allowed to act on them without some form of punishment. Thus, it is reasonable to conclude that women also have the same ability to be funny when they are not being punished socially for their joking behaviours. Women's humorous voices have been suppressed for centuries to create societies in which men appear wittier, more competent, and, thus, more desirable to women. But this is only a cultural norm; it can change, and it is changing.[19]

When the culture of men's assumed superiority gets its clown shoes off women's necks, women will be perceived as equally funny and not a threat to men when being funny. Women will be perceived as equally funny because they are equally as funny. Women are not political by nature until granted their freedom to be active citizens of the polis. Women are not as rational or intelligent as men by nature until they are given a proper education and take their place in the academic community. Women are not funny by nature until they are handed the microphone and given a chance to suffer diarrhea in the middle of the road in a wedding dress. Thank you, *Bridesmaids*.

Sorry to be such a lady-cuck, boys. I guess this essay was not really that funny,[20] so perhaps you would like to use that value judgment to tell me I am wrong?

Endnotes

1. Why can't *South Park* just make poo jokes?!

2. For more, see *Reddit* threads on *Rick and Morty* on this issue. But for your emotional safety, please do not.

3. Given the list of writing experience the female writers have under their bras, this is an accurate statement by Roiland.

4. In July 2018, an alt-right group on the website *4chan* attacked Harmon for what was dubbed an "obscene" sketch he performed in 2009, shaming Harmon and causing him to close his *Twitter* account. The harassment of writers on the show continues and is not only directed at the women. See Julia Alexander's *Polygon* article for more.

5. See also CNN, "The History of Comedy."

6. I suppose women, trying to affirm their right to vote, may not find your joke about denying them that right very funny.

7. To take credit for the joke.

8. Also, did you know that due to women's fear of losing her young, more women fall prey to the allure of the magic power of crystals? Hitchens may be right: I have one in my vagina right now.

9. Stanley also reports in her article how, nowadays, women are required to be near-supermodel looking to be considered for the role of a funny woman on television and film.

10. The article reads like Hitchens hitting on every woman who criticizes him and strongly implies that every woman who criticizes him does so out of desire for him.

11. This is a very brief and simplified version of the idea of frames of mind and mental spaces (for more, see Hurley, Dennett, and Adams 93-176; Minsky, *Society of the Mind* 243-59).

12. Hurley, Dennett, and Adams give a similar example, but I cannot help but use this from the geniuses at *Cyanide and Happiness.*

13. Hurley, Dennett, and Adams share a few examples of benign first-person mirth producing epistemic commitment errors, but I would like to add one of my own: honking your car horn at an automatic gate when it is closing on your car, somehow expecting the gate to hear your car horn and change its behaviour.

14. Sexual pleasure is not guaranteed for most women.

15. How active inferences come to be and how they are framed, as well as stored as data, are important issues but will not be expanded upon in this chapter.

16. "Super-normal stimuli" is a term evolutionary biologists use to describe any stimulus that elicits a specific reaction stronger than the stimulus for which it evolved to experience, such as the herring gull example in Tinbergen's 1953 book, *The Herring Gull's World.*

17. Citing Provine's research to make this point.

18. For more on this topic, see Genevieve Lloyd's *Man of Reason* (1984) and Lise Eliot's *Pink Brain, Blue Brain* (2010).

19. Anyone who has seen the work of Tina Fey, Wanda Sykes, Ali Wong, and Melissa McCarthy (to name a few) knows it is changing.

20. Yes, it was.

Works Cited

@nihilist_arbys. "There's No God So Why Not Worship Our Smokehouse Brisket? You'll Literally Get the Same Results." *Twitter* 20 Jan. 2015, twitter.com/nihilist_arbys/status/5576419557 32369 408. Accessed 23 Dec. 2020.

Alexander, Julia. "Rick and Morty's biggest subreddit is cracking down on trolls, abusive behavior." *Polygon*, 19 Oct. 2017, www.polygon.com/ 2017/10/19/16504250/rick-and-morty-reddit-trolls-harassment. Accessed 30 Dec 2020.

Congreve, William. "Concerning Humour in Comedy." *Theories of Comedy*, edited by Paul Lauter, Doubleday, 1964.

DenBleyker, Rob. "Cyanide and Happiness." *Explosm*, 22 Feb 2016, explosm.net/comics/4218/. Accessed 23 Dec.

Dockterman, Eliana. "These Are Joan Rivers' Best One-Liners." *Time*, 4 Sept 2014, time.com/3270645/joan-rivers-dead-one-liners/. Accessed 23 Dec. 2020.

Eliot, Lise. *Pink Brain, Blue Brain: How Small Differences Grow Into Troublesome Gaps—and What We Can Do about It.* Houghton Mifflin Harcourt, 2009.

Gajewski, Ryan. "'Rick and Morty' Co-Creators on Finale's Challenges, Hiring Female Writers, 'Community' Lessons." *The Hollywood Reporter* 3 Oct. 2015, www.hollywoodreporter.com/live-feed/rick-morty-creators-finales-challenges-828683. Accessed 23 Dec. 2020.

"The History of Comedy." *CNN*, 4 Jan. 2017, www.cnn.com/shows/history-of-comedy. Accessed 23 Dec. 2020.

Hitchens, Christopher. "Why Women Aren't Funny." *Vanity Fair*, Jan. 2007, www.vanityfair.com/culture/2007/01/hitchens200701. Accessed 23 Dec. 2020.

Hitchens, Christopher. "Why Women Still Don't Get It." *Vanity Fair*, Apr. 2008, www.vanityfair.com/culture/2008/04/hitchens200804. Accessed 23 Nov. 2020.

Hurley, Matthew, et al. *Inside Jokes: Using Humour to Reverse Engineer the Mind.* MIT Press, 2011.

Kazan, Olga. "Plight of the Funny Female: Why People Tend to Appreciate Men's Humour More than Women's." *The Atlantic*, 19 Nov. 2015, www.theatlantic.com/health/archive/2015/11/plight-of-the-funny-female/416559/. Accessed 23 Dec. 2020.

Lloyd, Genevieve. *The Man of Reason: "Male" and "Female" in Western Philosophy.* University of Minnesota Press, 1984.

Minsky, Marvin. *The Society of the Mind.* Simon and Schuster Press, 1988. Print.

Moss, Gabrielle. "A Brief History of Women Aren't Funny." *Bitch Media*, 29 Apr. 2013, www.bitchmedia.org/post/a-brief-history-of-women-arent-funny. Accessed 23 Dec. 2020.

Nopussy_ona_pedestal. "The Downfall of Rick and Morty, Thanks to Female Writers." *Reddit*, 14. Aug 2017, www.reddit.com/r/MGTOW/comments/6tkaf8/the_downfall_of_rick_and_morty_thanks_to_female/. Accessed 23 Dec. 2020.

Provine, Robert. *Laughter: A Scientific Investigation*. Penguin, 2001.

Saraiya, Sonia. "Harassment of Women Flows from Harvey Weinstein to 'Rick and Morty' Trolls." *Variety*, 18 Oct. 2017, variety.com/2017/tv/columns/harvey-weinstein-rick-and-morty-harassment-1202593673/. Accessed 23 Dec. 2020.

Stanley, Alessandra. "Who Says Women Aren't Funny?" *Vanity Fair*, April 2008, www.vanityfair.com/news/2008/04/funnygirls2008 04. Accessed 23 Dec. 2020.

Chapter Two

Phenomenology of a Feminist Joke and the Quintessential Emotional Labour in Maria Bamford's Comedy

Natalja Chestopalova

"Maria is an alternative comedian. As in, alternative to funny"
—*Lady Dynamite* S1:Ep.4

What does it mean to be an alternative comedian, and why are female comedians considered alternative? How and why does comedy thrive when a femme comedian takes over a humorous narrative and incites laughter? What sets the femme feminist comedian apart from other entertainers and their storytelling? And what kind of immersive emotional labour is involved in the femme comedian's work of making people laugh?

Maria Bamford's television series and stand-up comedy have carved out a space for the working through of such questions, including the difficulty of being a femme comedian in an industry that exhibits a prevalence towards silencing different and marginalized perspectives. Comedy, joking, and laughter are vital methods of cultural production that exist at the intersection of oral narrative techniques, social taboos, problematic industry practices, and changing media formats. The socially shared experience of comedy is part and parcel of a collaborative and evolving set of critical questions that can help us locate new ways of creating subversive femme narratives. Within these conversations, a self-identifying femme is defined not through gender but rather through the work of subverting the expectations they have to face for reclaiming queerness in all of its diversified forms and practices. Comedy is about sharing the difficulty of laughing about both the collective cultural contexts and the intimate, unconscious, and hidden inner complexities of being human. A good feminist joke that incites laughter is nothing less than a confession that there are still questions to be formulated about what narratives are prevalent, what voices are absent, what issues remain taboos, and what kinds of activist emotional labour remain vital. As comedian Hannah Gadsby notes in one of her stand-up performances, now is the right time to be questioning "this whole comedy thing" (*Nanette*).

This chapter focuses on some of the reasons why Bamford's work resonates with audiences by taking an inspired as well as a transparent stance against the excessive emotional labour involved in the creation of culturally specific and intersectional comedy. In an industry where women comedians have been "abused, discredited, blacklisted, turned into punch lines and driven out" (West), Bamford is claiming a space for activist perspectives and humour that want to talk about the sustainability of an empowered femme comedian. By taking a closer look at Bamford's comedic skits and series, including *Lady Dynamite* (2016–2017, Netflix), this chapter suggests that her works are an embodiment of recovering an intersectional feminist agenda that works against the normalization of feminism-as-commodity while being an unapologetic exercise in the creative process, which has the potential to double as activism. Bamford's work as an actor and a stand-up comedian is an example of feminist humour that revels in failure as a regenerative platform for addressing ageism, racism, sexism, addiction, and mental wellness.

Created by Pam Brady and *Arrested Development*'s Mitch Hurwitz, *Lady Dynamite* is much more than a "giddy comedy of mental challenges and spiritual optimism" (Lloyd) that came together as a fortuitous collaboration between Bamford and Netflix. This show is a product of Bamford's semifictionalized biography in conjunction with the desire to resist the longstanding climate of dismissiveness towards female comedians and especially towards female comedians suffering from what Bamford identifies as a "full-time chronic illness" ("The First Time

Someone Loved Me"). Some of *Lady Dynamite*'s reviews at the time of its release suggested that the show "risks alienating" its viewers and "truly doesn't care if you get it or not" (Famke)—a perception brought on by its metatextual elements concerned with the nature of Hollywood and the process of creating TV shows. Beyond its overemphasized self-referential humour and the constant breaking of the fourth wall, *Lady Dynamite* is a show about the character of Maria assessing her capacity to deal with OCD and type II bipolar disorder while balancing a career in comedy. The introduction to the pilot episode is a fitting indication of the tone and focus of Bamford's series:

> [Maria, using her "rich lady" Diane voice]: Single, stylish, now. A lady's got to be ready for when it happens. It's my life. And I'll do whatever it takes to get that sassafras feeling. Sassafras. Because when you feel this good... Ain't no man gonna tell me I ain't a woman.

> [Maria, using her regular voice]: "I'm a forty-five-year-old woman, who's clearly sun damaged. My skin is getting softer, yet my bones are jutting out, so I'm half soft half sharp. And I have a show! What a great late-in-life opportunity."

The pilot episode is the key to the series' multilayered agenda to entertain, educate, and further problematize the sustainability of an empowered femme comedian. One of the techniques established in the pilot is the colour coding of three different points in time, each one a rollercoaster of wit and complex emotional challenges. In the segments introduced as "The Past," Bamford is an emblem for frenetic success, living in Los Angeles with an unsustainably successful career and symptoms of hyperactivity setting her up for a mental-health breakdown. In the "Duluth" segments, Maria is with her parents in Minnesota, checking in and out of psychiatric facilities; these segments are explicit about the difficulty of recovery and the strain chronic mental illness can put on familial relationships. In "The Present" segments, Maria is back in Los Angeles and trying to prevent another breakdown as she reflects on the ethics behind some of her decisions in the past. The first post-breakdown meeting with her manager Bruce Ben-Bacharach tiptoes around the strain of understanding or defining success within the entertainment industry's culture of exploitation:

[Bruce]: The prodigal son returns! I can't believe you've been away for six whole months. So, tell me how do you feel? Are you refreshed? Revitalized? Renewed?

[Maria]: Yes, I do. I feel, uh … I feel very good, a little tired, uh … because of the heavy meds. But I'm also back on carbs. I'm eating pancakes, uh, almost all day.

[Bruce]: Well, the entire entertainment industry has been eagerly awaiting your glorious return.

[Maria]: Well…

[Bruce]: Now that you are back in town you tell me exactly what you want to do. TV shows, movie, world comedy tour … and I'm going to take a real shot at getting it for you. Uh, Chantrelle! Get me the hidden big opportunities list, would you?

[Maria]: Okay, I would like to do less, not more. That's the thing, could it be less ambitious? Or maybe not ambitious, anymore.

[Bruce, dictates to himself]: Less ambitious. No work for Maria. So that makes my job easier.

This encounter is one of many instances in *Lady Dynamite* where Maria finds herself in a position in which she needs to engage in the emotional labour of explaining or justifying her physical and affective needs. It is also a foreshadowing of the many conversations Maria will have to have with her managers, therapists, and even friends, during which she needs to defend her failure as a potentially regenerative space where "wellness is a process" (*Lady Dynamite* S1:Ep.2) rather than a quantifiable and commodifiable asset. These relationships are predatory insofar as they pressure Maria into taking on the emotional labour of suppressing genuine affective states, failing to manage legitimate concerns, and actively manifesting high functionality.

The pilot episode highlights the constructed nature of the juxtaposition between the femme performer's self-care and her stand-up career success. This contrast is made all the more visible through the pilot's repeated pseudo-comedic focus on Maria's legitimacy as a feminist stand-up comedian and her decision to use comedy as a narrative device in the series. The show's explicit use of misogynistic undertones takes on an almost exhausting quality as Maria is triggered into anxiety and self-doubt by a general lack of acceptance surrounding her work as a comedian and an actress. The themes of resilience and regenerative failure are constant in the series, as even her closest friend and assistant, Larissa, makes certain that she is regularly reminded that "Men are way funnier than women" (*Lady Dynamite* S2:Ep.3). In a cameo in the pilot episode, Patton Oswalt warns Maria against doing stand-up comedy and induces an almost apologetic reservation, as she publicly admits, "I'm not supposed to do comedy"; in fact, she says, "Let's not call it comedy; let's call it neighbour talk" (*Lady Dynamite* S1:Ep.1). There seems to be no escape from this constant emotional labour of existing and performing in a climate of toxic masculinity. For instance, in the second season, we find Maria being told by a seventeen-year-old teenager, Mikey J, to "sharpen" her material, to which she responds, "Yeah, that's what I need is, like, a seventeen-year-old-male perspective" (*Lady Dynamite* S2:Ep.3). This is, however, the problematic climate within which Bamford's show and femme comedy in general have to persist as well as thrive.

Writing about the comedy community, Lindy West notes that greater public awareness of toxic masculinity and rape culture, exemplified by comedians like Louis C.K. and Bill Cosby, only partially highlights the problems facing female comedians today. The industry has long sustained the structure of a boys' club where, as Jon Stewart has been known to say, "feminists can't take a joke" (West) and "straight male comedians, bookers and club owners have always been the gatekeepers of upward mobility" (West). There is a degree of pathology within these behaviours, from narcissism and self-loathing to normalization of abuse and sexual assault. The questions to ask here are: How does *Lady Dynamite* and Bamford's stand-up comedy fit into this discussion and what do they contribute to the recovery of a more inclusive and intersectional agenda?

What arguably hides at the core of discriminatory attitudes and abusive practices within the comedy and stand-up community is a lack of awareness about its innately gendered power dynamics, the structural inequality within the industry, and the resistance to systemic change. Part of the problem may lie in the fact that comedy and stand-up communities lack an implicit set of understandings that come so naturally to intersectional feminist perspectives. Ann Denis argues that these assumptions can and should be defined as certainties if they are to be helpful for our understanding of discrimination and the delegitimization of femme labour in comedy and beyond. According to Denis, these basic assumptions are that "women are legitimate subjects," that women are "socially constructed (as men are) rather than biologically determined," and that "as a social category, they have been subject to subordination" (678). The elimination of this subordination is of particular urgency and is directly dependent on the entertainment industry's collective and individual commitment to social change. Bamford's comedy and the semibiographical character of Maria further situate this individual commitment to change within the context of issues that are interdependent and, as such, are more difficult to grasp as part of a comedic creative process.

In order to identify some of the ways in which Bamford's comedy promotes intersectional and feminist perspectives, it is necessary to first accept that the unapologetic creative process of a femme comedian is itself a potential kernel for activism. It is also important to acknowledge that Bamford performs from a position of privilege, which informs how her comedy is written, received, and critiqued. A joke she often includes in her stand-up material summarizes this privileged perspective: When asked how she succeeds in her work as a comedian, she responds, "with a modicum of effort and every possible advantage" (*Old Baby*). This is a critical point of reference, since it is impossible to begin a conversation about the intersectional feminist agenda in comedy without acknowledging that there are sociopolitical economies always-already shaping performance as a practice.

The inclusion and discussion of intersectionality in Bamford's stand-up comedy and *Lady Dynamite* series occur in both implicit and explicit ways, which depend on a nuanced reading of comedy as a method of cultural memorialization and critique. Psychoanalyst and theorist Mladen Dolar writes that laughter coincides with "quintessential humanity" (29) and is a cultural product that exceeds language in both presymbolic and symbolic dimensions. There is an enigmatic quality to laughter because as a reaction to comedy, it "bursts out uncontrollably" and "seizes" (29) the subject at their most receptive, vulnerable, and unconscious. Comedic narratives and their respective receptions are, thus, intricate phenomena saturated with affect and capable of sustaining a transformative, alternative, and/or activist influence. However, this conversation cannot happen without a comprehensive definition of "intersectionality" that separates this concept from its limited token applications and instead invests it with the urgency and expansiveness with which it is entitled.

Defending the relevance of intersectionality as a framework for theorizing and critiquing varying types of identity, marginalization, and oppression, Kathryn T. Gines provides a definition in which the concept refers to the "multiple, interconnected layers of existence and identity," which include but are not limited to "the existential, political, social, and personal—and ranging from race, class, gender, sexuality, nationality, ethnicity, culture, and religion, to one's own relationship with oneself and others" (275). The expansive scope of Gines's definition of intersectionality and the way it perforates the social fabric is indicative of the challenge feminist artists, writers, and comedians face when it comes to the task of talking about issues of racism, ageism, and sexism. As Gines adds, "We live multiplicitous, intersectional, interconnected, and interdependent existences—our identities often operating in complex power relations with others" (275). This expanded definition is particularly valuable in relation to popular culture narratives, including television series and comedies, as they habitually reflect discriminatory practices and the industry's resistance to change.

Bamford's stand-up comedy and her semi-autobiographical role in *Lady Dynamite* attempt to recover a degree of this intersectional agenda through a series of storytelling arcs that focus on the power economies of ageism, sexism, racism, addiction, and mental health. If not explicitly concerned with intersectionality, Bamford, nonetheless, actively examines its basic assumptions that "power relations are about people's lives, how people relate to one another, and who is advantaged or disadvantaged within social interactions" (Collins and Bilge 7). Bamford's willingness to scrutinize her own experience within the entertainment industry is almost an activist response to the fact that mass-media spectacles always "serve political ends" (Collins and Bilge 11). In fact, the specificity of her storytelling arcs showcases a type of phenomenological approach to intersectionality or at least an attempt at intersectional comedy that is hyperconscious of the power economies in place and the emotional labour involved.

Phenomenological approaches to cinematic, theatrical, and performative narratives demonstrate an interest in a deeper specialized investigation of the formation and structure of personal and cultural experiences through conscious subjectivity. As such, phenomenological approaches to narratives are based on the repeated process of isolating specific types, affects, and aspects of being in the world (Husserl 60-85). Phenomenology in stand-up comedy and television series can assemble an analysis that attempts to explicate, or at least capture, the complex structures of affective experiences. Husserl's notion of "phenomenological bracketing" (135-139), or epocé, is relevant here as it is concerned with uncovering how a cinematic narrative can actively bracket the audience and direct them to focus on perceiving problematic affective experiences—including trauma, anxiety, depression, fear, or grief—within the deceptively familiar setting of a television series or stand-up performance. With bracketing in mind, the idea of feminist intersectionality, and the ways in which cinematic and performative media forms can capture it, intersectional comedy becomes even more exciting, as it offers a kind of active methodology for thinking about comedy as a tool of cultural production and critique.

On conscious and unconscious levels, Bamford's work is an active site for asking difficult questions about ageism, sexism, and racism as well as for destigmatizing mental illness and the various ways that a chronic condition can affect one's daily life and relationships. Bamford narrows in on these questions through a systemic, almost obsessive, dedication to the discussion of the forms and practices discriminatory and marginalizing perspectives can take. For example, she uses her age as part of a stand-up routine: "Yes! That is the perfect description of what I am. Very old and babylike" (Old Baby). Questions of age, aging, and ageism are also part of Bamford's extensive stand-up segments, as she impersonates her mother, adopting her mannerisms in a way that offers a rather positive and regenerative take on aging and the value of generational bonds. In a New York Times interview about becoming her mother on stage, Bamford discusses the positive effects this impersonation had on her mother and herself. She admits that through the embodiment of her mother's mannerisms and her own richer engagement with age, the experience of aging became more complex, elaborate, and enjoyable. Bamford habitually comments on age and aging, and how they can be, and already are, used to discriminate when it comes to appearance, employability, psychology, and social milestones, such as marriage and reproduction. One of her regular stand-up jokes that made it into the Lady Dynamite pilot takes a stab at reproduction when Maria announces,

"I just had my tubes tied. At my age, it's not safe to have children" (*Lady Dynamite*Sl:Ep.1). Working in an industry where youth and reproductive potential are approached as a commodity, Bamford is refreshingly candid and supportive of the need to dismantle age and aging as a secretive and shameful limitation instead of an enriching and shareable human experience.

Bamford's jokes about aging are intimately linked to her material on gender bias and sexist frameworks within the entertainment industry. Both seasons of *Lady Dynamite* feature ample examples of aggressive misogyny and discrimination against women in general and specifically in relation to femme feminist comedians. The pilot episode is indicative of the stressful working environment where feminist comedians have to perform while being marginalized, dismissed, and micromanaged. A recurrent series of jokes in *Lady Dynamite* is based on Maria's attempts to get cast in or act in a number of television shows based on misogynistic and discriminatory premises. In an episode titled "Bisexual Because of Meth," Maria gets cast in a sitcom named *Baby on Board*, in which her role as a secretary in a room full of male executives and one baby CEO quickly spirals out of control when the character played by the baby comments on her age and calls her breasts "dust bags" that cannot produce milk (Sl:Ep.2). Maria is quick to respond with a witticism of her own:

[Maria, addressing the baby CEO]: Just because you're a baby doesn't make that okay. You're just an adorable representation of misogyny. Let's lock you in a room for twelve hours with no food and you'd be begging for these slammin' mammary jammers.

[Maria, turning to the producers]: You okay with this? Hiding your sexist agenda behind these cute, chubby cheeks? I got no problem with this baby. You're just caught in the system, and that, my tiny little friend is the banality of evil! Hannah Arendt, look it up! (Sl:Ep.2)

After a moment of comedic triumph on set, Maria is equally excited to share her feminist victory with manager Bruce:

[Maria]: I felt great! And you were right about adlibbing. It's like I can be in a dumb, sexist show, but Trojan-horse it, you know? Criticize from within.

[Bruce]: Absolutely. That's it. You spoke the truth to power.

[Maria]: Yeah!

[Bruce]: And power fired you.

[Maria]: "What? They fired me? Why?

[Bruce]: "Well, to quote them exactly, they said they hate everything about you. They hate your humour, and your physicality, and ... your stupid fucking face." (S1:Ep.2)

After Maria is promptly fired, adding insult to injury, she is not allowed to go home but instead is forced to finish out the day. In many ways even more sinister than *Baby On Board*, one of the other television shows that cause Maria to engage in forced emotional labour—as she experiences a mixture of dread, anxiety, and disgust—is called *Lock Up a Broad*. In his pitch to Maria, her manager describes it as a show where women "are put inside a box and then they have an opportunity to apologize to a spouse or a lover, for valuable grand prizes," which shines "a whimsical light on the very real problem of female slavery" (*Lady Dynamite*S1:Ep.4). Although Maria admits that it is in fact an explicitly misogynistic show, she is pressured into participating and must use the emotionally draining as well as addictive "Diane voice" of a natural extrovert. At one point, Maria jokes that using the Diane voice makes her feel as if her own "shrill voice" is "almost a disability" (S1:Ep.4).

Bamford's character explicitly attempts to promote an intersectional feminist perspective in "White Trash," an episode almost entirely dedicated to the conversation about race and the interdependent power dynamics at the core of racism as a practice. "White Trash" is a vivid embodiment of phenomenological bracketing in so far as it cinematically tries to expose the intersecting affective economies of anxieties, fears, and trauma generated and sustained by racism. The episode begins with Maria being invited sans audition to play a part on a show called *White Trash*, which her manager Bruce promises will fulfill her requirements to have "more diversity in her life" (S1:Ep.3). Bruce likewise makes a point to refer to the show as a "Black show," in which "the leads are these two Black comics you can't tell one from the other" because they are twins Kenny and Keith Lucas, he quickly adds. On set, Maria begins to question whether it is racially insensitive to be part of this show by asking her costar Jennipher Nickles, played by Mila Sorvino, the following: "I was wondering, does this show make you uncomfortable? I mean the two lead minority characters are playing garbage people, and then all the producers are white. I've been out of the swing of things for a little while, but it seems a little demeaning. Is that weird? I mean, are we sellouts?" (S1:Ep.3). Concerned about being part of a show that normalizes racial discrimination and being viewed as a racist, Maria has to come to terms with her own feelings on the ethics of accepting work that is implicitly and intersectionally discriminatory. The exhausting emotional labour involved in this process of self-analysis becomes overwhelming and she ends up attending a meeting of the group Los Angeles People United for Racial Equality. The group consists of white people contemplating their own dangerously superficial and dismissive understanding of race and racism. The guidebook given out at the meeting is ominously titled *Minding My Own Business: The Premier Guide to Innocuous Race Relations* and echoes the advice given to Maria to filter her conversations using the mantra "If you're white, keep it light" (S1:Ep.3). The "White Trash" episode concludes with a sense of disappointment for Bamford as a feminist and ally when she announces that "We said a lot of important things about race," even though the episode itself "didn't solve anything" (S1:Ep.3). A cameo by John Ridley, the Academy-Award-winning screenwriter of *12 Years a Slave*, confirms Maria's failure as an ally when he refuses to engage in the emotional labour of unpacking race and racism for her and the audience: "I wish I could help you on this one, but you're on your own," adding "I don't think what you're doing is malicious, it's just recklessly ignorant" (S1:Ep.3). The episode does manage to critique the dangers of comedies that sustain an ambiguous attitude towards racism as part of the multiplicity of power economies that discriminate and marginalize. Ridley's disapproval of how Maria handled the conversation about racism pinpoints an emotional duality, in which the failure to critically address racism can come in a variety of forms. "White Trash" shows a dual anxiety about racism—one solipsistic and superficial and the other an almost existential anxiety, which can only be addressed through legitimate responsibility, compassion, and transparency.

In *Lady Dynamite*, the discussions of race and racism are closely tied to concerns with the implicit flaws of a capitalist mentality and the types of frenetic dynamics of exploitation they maintain. For instance, Maria's role as the face of Checklist department store, a reference to her real appearances in Target commercials, links capitalist rhetoric with exploitative and discriminatory practices in Mexico. The manic energy of the fictionalized Checklist commercials is evocative of the compulsion to ceaselessly consume and exploit. It is impossible to separate these interconnecting issues from Bamford's commitment to destigmatize mental illness and create a safe space for conversations about the long-term depression and agitated hypomania of bipolar II. *Lady Dynamite* is, after all, a show that is implicitly framed by a semiautobiographical narrative about living with mental illness rather than transcending its symptoms through miraculous cures, career achievements, or functioning relationships.

Bamford's acting work and stand-up comedy—especially the shows recorded with her parents and pugs as the only audience members in attendance—are an honest portrayal of the different types of emotional labour involved in feminist comedy. There is an intuitive sense of strength and almost activist honesty in writing and performing comedy as a self-healing and therapeutic practice. Comedy, stand-up, and other creative arts are a way to work through, deal with, manage, and, to some extent, understand mental illness and all of the emotional and physical demands it imposes. In *Lady Dynamite*, Maria is often pressured to "get off these fucking drugs!"(S1:Ep.11) and to instead exploit her manic energy at the cost of her health and relationships. Her comedy work narrows in and brackets the emotional experiences associated with such exploitation and the industry's well-established practice of perpetuating the stereotype that "all of the greats are unstable" (S1:Ep.11). The comedy industry, thus, both stigmatizes mental illness and abuses its manic aspects as fuel for creativity in neuroatypicals.

What sets the femme feminist comedian apart from other entertainers and their storytelling is the willingness to take on the exhaustive emotional labour involved in making people laugh while reflecting on key social issues. Beyond the Sisyphean task of resisting the pressures from the entertainment industry, a feminist comedian has to constantly work on the types of storytelling humour that are hyperconscious of the intersectional nature of discriminatory and marginalizing perspectives. This practice is also what makes a femme comedian an alternative one, since the toll of even trying to incite laughter while tackling established social practices is one of the quintessential acts of resistance. The sustainability of an empowered femme comedian depends on the entertainment industry's capacity to accept that it is inherently predicated on a multiplicity of interconnected biases and forms of discrimination. Due to the new production potential of streaming services and media formats, there is an ongoing push for changes that will empower rather than isolate the work of feminist comedians. Bamford's stand-up comedy and series like *Lady Dynamite* have the potential to create narratives about activism and intersectional thinking as well as provide a regenerative platform for storytelling that narrows in and brackets the compound affective economies of living with mental illness.

Works Cited

Bamford, Maria. *Lady Dynamite*, Season 1-2, Netflix Studios, 2016–2017.

Bamford, Maria. "Maria Bamford on Becoming Her Mother." *New York Times* (*YouTube* Channel), 21 July 21 2014, www.youtube.com/watch?v=WdNLGEDgdCA. Accessed 24 Dec. 2020.

Bamford, Maria. "Maria Bamford: The First Time Someone Loved Me for Who I Really Am." *The New York Times*, 31 Oct. 2017, www.nytimes.com/2017/10/31/arts/television/maria-bamford-lady-dynamite.html. Accessed 24 Dec. 2020.

Bamford, Maria. *Old Baby*, directed by Jessica Yu, Netflix Studios, 2017.

Berry, David. "In Lady Dynamite, Maria Bamford Finds Comedy in the Places Where You Would Least Expect It." *National Post*, 27 May 2016, nationalpost.com/entertainment/in-lady-dynamite-maria-bamford-finds-comedy-in-the-places-where-you-would-least-expect-it. Accessed 24 Dec. 2020.

Collins, Patricia Hill, and Sirma Bilge. *Intersectionality*. Polity Press, 2016.

Denis, Ann. "Intersectional Analysis: A Contribution of Feminism to Sociology." *International Sociology*, vol. 23, vol. 5, 2008, pp. 677-94.

Dolar, Mladen. *A Voice and Nothing More*. MIT Press, 2006. Print.

Gadsby, Hannah. *Nanette*, directed by Jon Old and Madeleine Parry, Netflix Studios, 2018.

Gines, Kathryn T. "Black Feminism and Intersectional Analyses." *Philosophy Today*, vol. 55, 2011, pp. 275-84.

Husserl, Edmund. *The Essential Husserl: Basic Writings in Transcendental Phenomenology*, edited by Donn Welton, Indiana University Press, 1999.

Lloyd, Robert. "One Crazy Journey: Maria Bamford Returns in the Real and Surreal 'Lady Dynamite.'" *Los Angeles Times*, 23 Nov. 2017, www.latimes.com/entertainment/tv/la-et-st-lady-dynamite-season-two-20171117-story.html. Accessed 24 Dec. 2020.

West, Lindy. "Why Men Aren't Funny." *The New York Times*, 14 Nov. 2017, www.nytimes.com/2017/11/14/opinion/louis-ck-not-funny-harassment.html. Accessed 24 Dec. 2020.

Chapter Three

I Have to Laugh, or I'll Die

Aba Amuquandoh

In the summer of 2014, it seemed as though I just couldn't catch a break. My maternal grandfather had just passed away, leaving my mother distraught and utterly exhausted. A dark cloud settled over my childhood home in Brampton, Ontario, that June, and as the visitors trooped in and out of my house to mourn with my mother, I couldn't help but wonder if they could see the sombre fog that followed my family and me. Apparently not, because every time my mother would begin to wail in grief for her beloved father, someone would make a joke. I was livid. I remember storming into my bedroom-cum-guest room in anger, and shoving my headphones in my ears so I could listen to Fiona Apple (my favourite artist to listen to when I'm depressed and the only white woman I trust) to drown out the sound of all my aunts and uncles joking and laughing at such a dark time for my family.

I woke up three hours later, with my laptop turned over on its side, my headphones wrapped around my neck, and my eyes still stinging from crying. As my eyes adjusted to my now-dark room, I heard a familiar peal of laughter erupting from the guest living room where everyone was situated that evening. It was my mother's familiar laughter intermingled with the shrieks and guffaws of my extended family. I was shocked, confused, and extremely angry; I couldn't believe how inappropriately everyone was behaving during this time of mourning.

I sulked downstairs and into the kitchen to find my mom replenishing snacks. She turned around and caught my eye, reached out and grabbed my hand. "What are you guys laughing about?" I asked grimly, befuddled as to how she could even stand to entertain guests at the moment. My mother loved her father very much; she would call him every day and remind him not to eat so much meat and to stop drinking and smoking so that he may live long. When guests came over my mom would entertain everyone with tales of my grandfather and his brothers getting up to hare-brained antics. These stories were my favourite, and I always keeled over from laughing so hard. This was my first big loss of a relative, and I couldn't muster up the courage to put forth a brave face, so I didn't understand how my mother, a woman who had spent a great deal of her adult life making sure her father was taken care of, could be seemingly okay in this moment. I couldn't understand how she could laugh in a moment like that. She held my hand, smiled, and said: "It's okay. They'll leave soon. It won't be loud for much longer. Go back to sleep." At that moment, I realized that my mother was also disturbed by my family's joyful and almost celebratory presence, but I assumed that she was just keeping a brave face in order to not offend her guests who had gathered to mourn the death of my grandfather.

A month after my grandfather's death, I suffered from a nervous breakdown. On my way to work one morning in July, I had one of the worst panic attacks of my life. I found myself gasping for air with my head hanging out the car window as it idled in a Tim Hortons' parking lot. The next day I quit my job, and I stayed in bed for two weeks. My father didn't know what to do with me, and my mother cried constantly. To make matters worse, my local family doctor had no clue what to do with my situation and prescribed me sleeping pills, which is absolutely not what you should prescribe someone suffering from depression. Those two weeks felt like an entire year, and I was extremely angry with myself.

Unable to understand why I was so overcome with this sadness I found myself leaning on old crutches. I contacted my friend from high school, Dana. She didn't like me when she first met me. She thought I was too loud and happy, especially at 9:00 a.m. in our high school gym class. Fair enough. I was an annoying and a strange fourteen year-old, but I don't know what I'd give to be that hopelessly happy and optimistic about life again. Dana got over her aversion to my happiness and we rapidly became friends, especially bonding on the basis that we were both Ghanaian. I believe that this, paired with our chaotic and bizarre shared sense of humour, is what made us work. We built a toxic relationship that was cemented by shared trauma and our dependence on humour as a coping mechanism. We often communicated through memes, expressing our annoyances and grievances towards our parents through a variety of peculiar and, quite frankly, disgusting content. They ranged from the then-popular (now Nazi mascot) Pepe the Frog memes to a horrible video of a 3D farmer named Tom R Toe singing to his plants beneath an overcast sky (please watch it on YouTube; it's still delightfully terrible). Dana and I spent countless evenings recounting embarrassing moments, sharing our anger about men, listening to music, and eating together. Our favourite thing to do was to scroll through our fangirl Tumblr pages on our laptops while sitting next to each other; we'd turn the screen towards the other every few moments to laugh at something horrible. There was something always eating at us back then—an internal nagging that we satiated with depression naps and cruel laughter.

Whatever was tugging at Dana caught up with her a bit sooner than it did with me. She fought with her parents and began to lie a lot. She didn't eat as much, and the brightness of her ludicrous sense of humour began to fade. She stopped coming to school as often and eventually began to decline my help and friendship. I became more serious about school in grade twelve, making me closer to my more studious friends as we studied hard and packed on as many extracurriculars as possible in hopes of making it into our university of choice. I began auditioning for theatre schools; I stayed late after school for extra coaching, spent more time writing content for my portfolio, and commuted to Toronto to take acting classes. As my real life became more packed with responsibility, my online presence dwindled, and I did not attend to my comedic Tumblr and Twitter accounts the way I used to. I graduated and left Brampton and Dana behind me.

During my first year at the University of Toronto, I did very well in my practical drama courses. I excelled in my theory classes, and I completed the term with a new set of friends and a new sense of independence. I delved into this new sense of adulthood by grocery shopping for myself, cooking my own food, and drinking wine with dinner. I was truly a child's image of an adult. I had a solid routine for the first few months, especially because everything felt shiny and new. Yet as it all fell into a steady pace, a feeling of monotony began to set in, and, of course, the differences between myself and my roommates began to show. First off, I was the only Black person in the apartment. This brought on the usual microaggressions about hair, food, colloquialisms, and music. When I used the Black slang I was so used to using and hearing, I was met with hostile confusion and eyes that could size me up and knock me down with the smugness with which it seems all white people are equipped. I hated myself after these experiences. In order to survive, I kept my distance from my roommates, and I swallowed all my doubts, fears, and anger. There was an insecurity about me that was highlighted by living with all those straight white women. I knew I did not belong for the obvious reasons such as race and class but also because something inside was setting me apart, and though it was inside of me, I felt like everyone could see it. This thing inside of me throbbed like a wound that had festered. So, I began to harbour a deep shame that echoed the feeling of aberrance with which I had trudged through so many of my high school years.

Dana had contacted me through Facebook at the beginning of that first year of university. We began to talk again, and she came to visit me at my residence that winter. I had missed her, I realized. I had missed our jokes, and I had missed how familiar she felt to me. The light of her friendship coming back into my busy and depressed life felt like the love for which I had been yearning. We saw each other every other weekend or so after that and fell back into a familiar routine. I told her all about the boys I had crushes on and about how I was tired and depressed and out of energy—and how I hated being the only one. She listened, and she understood, as she always did, because we always saw ourselves in each other.

By the end of the school year, I was gearing up to leave my residence to move back to Brampton and find a summer job. But it felt as though this tugging feeling did not stem from the fear of finding short-term work in my hometown. It felt stranger and greater than the standard anxiety that follows a student going back home to make some money before their next semester. It felt as though I was missing something integral to my being, almost as though I would look down at my body one day and find that both of my arms were gone. It didn't make sense to me at the time, so I buried the feeling the way I buried all of the feelings and thoughts that made me uncomfortable. I went back to Brampton.

Dana and I sat next to our bikes in a local park as we ate ice cream one August afternoon. She gulped down her last bite and threw the wrapper in her bag. "Yo, I'm gay," she proclaimed. Without missing a beat, I launched myself into an upright position, "Yo, me TOO!" I shouted. We laughed and settled into each other as we continued to lounge around on the grass. "I like lipstick lesbians," she said. "I like me a good butch," I laughed. "But I still like boys," I said as I munched on my last bite of ice cream. "Yuck, me too," she said as she yanked grass into her balled fists. Finally, we each had one foot out of the closet. And now when I think of our announcements, I know that we both already knew. We recognized the queerness in one another and never spoke it out loud due to fear of what others would say. The rest of that summer, I biked around Brampton with her; we'd hang out at her place and watch gay cult classics or nap at my house through whole afternoons. It was relaxing, but the air of melancholy still lingered over us. It was the source of our humour; we'd make dark jokes about how we'd have to kill ourselves if our parents found out we were queer. We used these jokes to subdue the anxiety that came with being in the closet. This humour was desperately needed. It kept me from folding into myself again, and it helped me work through all the noise that surrounded my newfound identity.

Dana and I remained friends until the following summer. Throughout the time we were friends, my interest in professional comedy grew, and this extension of myself matured. As I began taking gender studies courses at school, I began to understand what it is to be queer. I made more queer friends and gained a community that solidified my identity. I came to realize that I wasn't alone in my experiences. The precarity dissipated, and with that came a clarity that I hadn't known for quite some time. Being queer isn't hard and being queer isn't a source of anxiety or sadness; being subjected to a culture and system that is created to suppress and often kill you is hard. It is a source of anxiety and sadness to live in a home with parents who love you and want the best for you but who also do not understand what queerness is, or why you would ever burden yourself with that. Through the roller coaster of emotions that I have felt in my adult life, comedy has always allowed me to work through it and be open about it. I don't know if I would have discovered my queer identity if it wasn't for the freedom Dana and I were able to build for each other by making absurd, cathartic jokes that prompted us to laugh, learn, and take risks.

I have officially been a professional comic for a year now. I am so grateful to the mentors in Toronto who work hard to take care of new comedians, such as myself, and who create opportunities for work in this cutthroat industry. Such people as Celeste Yim, Coko Galore, Nelu

Handa, Anasimone George, and many others have been my guardian angels as I build my comedy career. For them, I am grateful.

I have been feeling nostalgic recently, so I have checked up on the friends that I don't keep in contact with. By checked up, I mean creeping on their social media profiles. It's strange for me because I'm usually good at keeping my distance from people who aren't in my life anymore. I stumbled upon Dana's profile one night after work; she looks very different. She looks stable and happy and much like the girl I first met a decade ago. Sailor Sad, my much loved (by me) Twitter account, has been upgraded from a shady and depressing shit-post account to a professional shit-post account where I happily share my identity and talk openly and candidly about my life experiences. Comedy has done far more for me than I could have ever imagined it would have done when I was just a kid.

I understand my mother better now. Looking back at my grandfather's passing, I realize that she needed that laughter and she needed that gathering of family to laugh with in order to get through one of the hardest times of her life. The laughter and stories that she experienced that night did not make the blow of losing her father any easier, but they did take her mind off it, even if only for a few hours. I now have a greater grasp of this type of coping mechanism; now, I understand how important it is to laugh as a queer Black woman as I approach my mid- twenties.

Chapter Four

"Man, That Guy's Sad... but He Killed": Survivors of Sexual Violence Joke about Rape

Anna Frey

It was May 2016, and I needed to laugh about rape. Joking can be cathartic—one reason we laugh is to spontaneously release pent-up tension. I needed that release, and I wasn't alone. Two stand-up comics living on the west coast of Canada, Heather Jordan-Ross and Emma Cooper, felt similarly: They'd organized a national tour that spring which brought comics to stages to tell stories and crack jokes about times that they themselves had been sexually assaulted or harassed. When I showed up to Comedy Bar in downtown Toronto for their second of two nights, a small crowd of mostly young and mostly-women was already anxiously texting or smoking on the sidewalk out front. Above us, the Comedy Bar marquee glowed, declaring "RAPE IS REAL." I laughed, delighted by their boldness and relieved by their honesty, and ducked my head and went inside.

By this time, I knew that laughing about rape was not only possible but overwhelmingly productive for me. Coming across Patricia Lockwood's poem "Rape Joke" years earlier had felt like making eye contact with an open-faced stranger across a crowded metro car— electric and humanizing but ultimately fleeting. Jessie Kahnweiler's short film *Meet My Rapist* gave me more evidence towards what was achievable: a different way of relating to sexual violence. It was a method of communicating trauma that felt more natural to me, connecting me to a community of other survivors making and appreciating similar content. I needed to laugh about rape because every other reaction felt stifling. Whether we notice them or not, discourses about rape pervade our everyday lives (Projansky 2). We hear about rape through news stories, true-crime reports, television and film, *Twitter* hashtags, and through any other media source we consume. These representations are largely encoded with similar themes and values: misogynist, victim-blaming rhetoric that shifts the responsibility for the violence from the perpetrator(s) to the survivor(s) (Fahs 65). These discourses are insidious, seeping into our consciousness and influencing our social relations. As Sarah Projansky writes within her project of unearthing the propagation of rape culture through cinema, "Discourses of rape are both productive and determinative. They are not simply narratives marketed for consumption in an entertainment context or 'talk' about real things. They are themselves functional, generative, formative, strategic, performative, and real" (2). Laughing at rape and rape culture therefore doesn't just offer a moment of relief for survivors and allies desperate for solidarity and recognition; it is an essential part of a larger feminist movement that is actively engaged in building a new and safer world.

This chapter grew from interviews I did with seven stand-up comics who had experience performing material about sexual violence they themselves had survived (Frey). They are each referred to here by pseudonyms. I am indebted to their knowledge, guts, and willingness to be reflective and vulnerable with me. The scaffolding of theory I have built around their work is meant to honour their voices and tie them in to larger sociocultural and political schemas.

My curiosity about expanding the roster of feelings allowed to people who have survived sexual violence developed from both cultural theorist Raymond Williams's "structure of feeling" and trauma theorist Ann Cvetkovich's "archive of feelings." Williams helps us understand systemic power as flexible and socially constructed through his attention to "meanings and values as they are actively lived and felt" in everyday life by everyday people (132). Cvetkovich writes of "trauma cultures," people brought together through cultural initiatives with trauma as their focus. Her archive of feelings is "an exploration of cultural texts as repositories of feelings and emotions, which are encoded not only in the content of the texts themselves but in the practices that surround their production and reception" (7). Taken together these perspectives on feelings remind us that our emotional lives are intuitive indicators of our relationship to current mechanisms of power. Cultural interventions, such as Rape Is Real and Everywhere, offer moments that can jolt us into clearer consciousness. For me, one jolt came as I read the marquee above Comedy Bar: Had I ever seen such a blunt and vibrant public acknowledgement that rape exists? Have you?

Simone, one of the comics I spoke with, highlighted the isolation that many survivors experience: "You always feel so alone in it. You can tell your friends and family and talk to your therapist and stuff, but you still feel really alone in it, and to be with people who knew exactly what you were going through ... was really, really awesome." Despite having a solid and generous support network, Simone still felt emotionally alone until she connected in person with other survivors. Unfortunately, due largely to the social stigma or further violence that survivors can face if we choose to publicly disclose our experiences, building relationships with other survivors is often difficult to orchestrate. Outside of rape crisis centres, survivor support organizations, and annual Take Back the Night marches, survivors are typically invisible and presumed nonexistent. The comedy club offers an alternative space for this trauma culture to form. It's far less exposed than a rape crisis centre, in that you've got plausible deniability should your auntie spot you walking in. It's low pressure for audience members, since comedy conventions of laughing, clapping, and cheering for performers supplant the otherwise complex emotional demands of responding to disclosures of sexual violence, and the club provides a structure for performers and crowds alike to engage with one another about sexual violence during and after the show in a spirit of camaraderie, good humour, and fun. Lisa, a comedian, said the following:

> At the end of the show, it was really nice to have people come up to me; a few women were like, "Hey, can I give you a hug?" People identified as survivors or said that my experience specifically spoke to them. I had a few Facebook messages later too, and that had never happened to me before. So that was, from a selfish perspective, immensely gratifying because one of the reasons, the main reason I like comedy, or what I want to do with my comedy, is [to] reflect people's experiences back to them and give a voice to that. It was nice to finally be able to do that.

Lisa had mentioned earlier in our conversation that she had initially been reluctant to perform on a sexual violence–themed show, since her experience of violence was, in her words, "a minor-ish sexual assault" and she didn't want to offend any potential audience members who had had "really horrendous experiences." Rape culture functions to silence and isolate survivors to the point where many of us haven't been able to contextualize our experiences within a larger political schema. Coming to understand all acts of sexual violence as related under the same systems of domination and oppression is a step towards building solidarity between survivors and allies. As Lisa learned during and after her set, not only did audience members not lash out at her, but many also thanked her for sharing and told her that parts of her story resonated deeply with them. Moments like these were common for many of the performers I spoke with. The following quote from Nancy illustrates how her set was a turning point for several audience members:

> Once I've talked about sexual assault, I've had people come up to me afterwards and have those private conversations where they say, "Your particular situation ... is exactly what happened to me." So, I did get on the tour a lot of people who came to say, "Yeah, I just had this grey thing, and I didn't know that I could call it that, so thanks for saying that because I never would have known.' And then you're like, "oh, okay, this is a thing that happens to a lot of people," I can go forward and say that joke with more confidence, in a way. So, you're almost seeing the gears of understanding and learning turning through those conversations."

Like Lisa above, Nancy is referring to her experience of sexual violence as something relatively minor; in her case, she uses the language of "greyness" to convey this. Rather than looking at consent as a black or white concept, she integrates the idea of shades of grey into her routine in order to encompass a more realistic scope of sexual violence that includes such acts as coercive sex, secretly removing a condom partway through sex, agreeing to one sex act and then being pressured into another, among many other potential situations. These behaviours are often written off as misunderstandings, and survivors are accused of overreacting if we complain about them too loudly or insistently. Nancy refused to be complicit in this hierarchy of violence. Through her set, she created a feedback loop between herself and audience members in which they both gained confidence to name their experiences as real assaults.

Although the benefits of survivors bearing witness to the histories of other survivors are substantial, the experience doesn't come without associated risks. Although it can be liberatory for a survivor to learn that they are not alone and that the violence they have experienced is connected to larger schemas, that same knowledge can alternatively be interpreted as pointing towards a demoralizing and insurmountable situation (Brison, "Everyday" 193). The following quote from Katie describes her emotions after performing at a run of sexual violence-themed shows:

> I had a friend pick me up to take me to where I was staying, and I was just [weeping], "The world is a horrible place and everyone's in pain," and she was like, "No, you're just in a really specific context and that's a small version of the population," and I was like, "It's so many more than you ever think." It's just a lot. It's a lot. On one hand, it's like, "You're not alone!' But then it's like, "You're not alone." I say this in my act, too. I wish that I could be the only person because I can handle it. I wish that I can be the only person that this ever happened to, you know? So that no one else would have to go through it.

This conversation Katie had with her friend happened after she had been approached by a stream of audience members wanting to confide in her about how meaningful they had found her performance. Earlier in our conversation, she had mentioned, "Usually after I perform, I like to hide; I don't like talking to people afterwards." For reasons outside of her control, she was unable to leave the venue in time to avoid the people who wanted to speak with her, resulting in a breach of her boundaries and a loss of personal agency. Katie's honesty in sharing this distressing series of events reminds us that care must be taken in any cultural initiative that deals with sexual violence to preserve the autonomy of all performers as well as that of members of the audience.

Katie's account was unique among the performers I spoke with. Although nearly everyone agreed that some parts of the writing process or the performances themselves were emotionally challenging, no one else articulated such an isolated moment of distress related to interactions with people who had seen their show. Overall, most of the comics were in line with Judith Lewis Herman's assessment of social action being an integral part of recovery for a "significant minority" of survivors (207). Herman refers directly to politics and religion as spheres on which survivors choose to focus their efforts, but, following Cvetkovich, I push for the inclusion here of cultural endeavours as another arena available to survivors interested in a more diffuse therapeutic process that pursues social as well as personal change. I give the final word on this topic to Nancy, who tells us about the times she spent drinking at clubs with fellow performers and audience members after her set:

> And then people having a beer after and just talking with people and just being reminded consistently that this happens to so many different kinds of people, [that] this isn't the main thing in anyone's life, and [that] everyone wants to just live their life and do their thing, but everyone is also willing to stop their life and really think about this, really put themselves out there, because they felt it was important—it was really cool.

Susan Brison, a philosopher and a survivor of attempted sexual murder, writes emphatically about how learning to tell the story about the violence she endured was a crucial component of her mental and emotional recovery (*Aftermath* 15). Like Herman, she underscores the importance of finding people willing to bear witness to these stories of violence (Brison, *Aftermath* 16; Herman 9). Despite their encouragement of narration, neither author considers the role that genre can play in a survivor's project of telling their own story. This hidden assumption that any recounting of sexual violence must be sombre, rageful, or teary reinforces the limited range of feelings socially permitted by survivors. Stand up comedy is one venue that offers an escape from these sometimes suffocating restrictions.

The following quip from Victoria illustrates the absurdity of policing survivors' affective lives: "I say [on stage] as well: 'I get it, I get it, if you're sensitive, don't come out to a show. Because why should someone who's had this worst thing to ever happen to them ever deserve to laugh again?'" She's referring here to other comics and comedy fans who complain that rape survivors are ruining stand up comedy culture by being oversensitive about and easily offended by misogynist rape jokes. In this framing, rape survivors are the problem, and the solution is for us to be excluded from the comedy scene. These allegations of humourlessness serve multiple purposes: They take discourses about rape out of survivors' mouths; they displace the responsibility for survivors' welfare from the community onto the individual; and, once again, they drive home the idea that survivors have neither the interest nor capacity to laugh about rape. This last attitude filters through culture and affects even well-meaning close relations of survivors. Here, Simone reflected on what she had learned after performing a set about her experience of assault: "That you can laugh about it, first of all. Every time you want to talk about it with a friend, it always feels so dire. Your friend is like, 'We need wine now!' It felt so intense. It was kind of nice to be able to laugh about it and take something really awful and make it not awful."

Comedy provided an alternative structure for Simone, where she got to experiment with speaking about trauma with emotions that were disallowed to her in her regular social circles. Cvetkovich writes that "Responses to trauma are often constrained by (normalizing) demands for appropriate affects" (26). These demands, as illustrated so far through the testimonies of my participants, are not in survivors' best interests. Cultural pressure to either be silent about the violence we have survived or to only speak of it with tears and wine, as was Simone's experience, contributes to humour and laughter being understudied and underused tools for living with and healing from sexual trauma.

The cognitive and linguistic principles involved in telling jokes about surviving sexual violence can encourage positive changes in how survivors perceive and process their experiences. One way through which this can happen is by using the relief theory of humour. This theory explains a particular kind of laughter—one we experience when we notice that an accepted norm has first been violated and then amended to its anticipated state. In other words, a stressor has been introduced, causing anxiety, but is then removed, and the quick dissipation of tension can often provoke laughter as people sense a return to normalcy. It can be a real victory for survivors to craft a narrative of their own that follows the cycle of relief humour: identifying the existence of a pre-traumatized self, locating the source of trauma, and alleviating some discomfort by reconceptualizing the situation. This type of narrative can make a "situation seem more elastic, or more manageable, by showing that difficulties are not so overwhelming as to be out of control after all"

(Meyer 312). Avery provided an example of a joke he tells mainstream audiences that demonstrates a successful attempt at reconceptualizing the trauma of childhood molestation: "I was molested when I was a kid; when I was five, I was molested a few times. One of my favourite jokes is 'I used to do really well for myself; back in the day, I used to pick up left and right as far as like, it's a dude a day, you know, but then I turned seven.' That usually goes over alright; people tend to like that."

This joke effectively identifies the desirable social norm of having an active and pleasurable sex life and then quickly contrasts it to the anxiety-inducing idea of applying that norm to young children. The relief is tied in with the punchline: Avery announcing that "but then I turned seven" clues the audience in to the fact that this sexual activity was happening to him as a child, but it also reveals that the abuse ended at that time. His presence on stage and his capacity to deliver the joke signal his survival. Writing a joke like this may encourage "an internal redefining of sociocultural reality," which helps a survivor to understand their trauma not as a life-ending event but as an experience that can be incorporated into their new reality more easily (Meyer 311). The joke above, like many stand-up comedy bits, relies on an element of surprise to be successful: Framing being molested in one's childhood as being successful at "picking up dudes" is an unexpected approach. This type of reworking traumatic memory requires remarkable cognitive labour. Not only does an author need to have developed a stable narrative of their trauma, but they also need to then hold that narrative in place and step back from it to consider it from different angles and affects in order to make new connections between elements they have previously considered disparate. Later in our interview, Avery acknowledged the potential benefits of writing comedy about sexual violence: "For sure, I'd like to say why I think it's important to write jokes in regards to it, just because … one of the most cathartic things to do, when you experience trauma, is to flip it and laugh at it. I always believe that the whole world is a joke, and it's either like, you laugh at it, or it's laughing at you."

Avery understands shifting perspectives as "flipping" assumptions on their heads in order to gain control and to laugh at what had previously been considered upsetting. We can consider Simone's quote above— where she describes writing comedy about her assault as "tak[ing] something really awful and mak[ing] it not awful"—in the same vein. These experiences are in line with Brison's assertion that saying something about a traumatic memory does something to that memory, but Avery and Simone help us understand that the manner in which something about the memory is said can influence what may happen to it (*Aftermath* 56). According to Avery, speaking humorously induces a more cathartic response from him than by speaking in any other mode. Humour's position within language grants it special permissions: Where ordinary descriptive or logical language runs up against boundaries and redundancies, humour is able to fill in some of the blanks. When language fails to adequately represent traumas we have experienced, we turn to adjectives like "indescribable, unspeakable, or inexpressible" to attempt to communicate the intensity of those actions or feelings (Jackson 210). More playful modes of speech invite metaphors and incongruities to the stage, so to speak. Comedic bits have the liberty to breach established boundaries, typical directions of thought, and assumed connections between ideas to introduce novel interpretations, definitions, and possibilities—all by encouraging more creative uses of language than those typically found in straightforward dialogue.

The most notable difference between humour and regular speech is the singular response humour invites: laughter. A successful comic will be able to orchestrate a crowd of laughers in unison. Laughter is often described as being contagious, but this is not strictly true. In the case of language-based humour, like most stand-up comedy, a person must follow and get the joke in order to really laugh. In other words, they must fulfill the conditions of being susceptible to humour; sitting in a room full of people laughing does not usually suffice. Getting the joke requires that an audience member share a knowledge base or ideological perspective with the performer: any number of intragroup ethnic jokes or inside jokes between friends can serve as an example here. Katie had this to say about the nature of laughter: "A lot of laughter ... [involves] you recognizing that something is funny "because me, too. Me, that, also, too.'" It is this ability to spontaneously identify a common value, understanding, or belief that allows us to think of laughter as a method of validating a comic's (fragmented, dislocated, and traumatized) memory. Similar to how "the invisible genome vouches for the validity of phenotype, or the effaced technologies of the photo argue the 'Fact' of its real representation" (Stevens 34), a burst of laughter opens the curtains to the piece of reality being mocked. If we look again at Avery's joke about childhood sexual abuse, we can see how this validation plays out: The joke is only successful if the audience recognizes that the widely accepted norm of not molesting children has been breached. Any listener who did not share this belief would not be prompted into feelings of surprise or relief when Avery delivered the punchline and would, therefore, fail to laugh.

Another example of this is provided by Lisa, who, as mentioned earlier, was nervous about participating in a comedy show about sexual violence because she didn't think that her experiences were severe enough to warrant her inclusion: "It was funny to get validated in that way and then to talk about that on stage. Like I joked about it on stage, feeling like, "Oh, but I wasn't like really raped,' and then giving [the assault] like a movie rating. People were really laughing and relating to that, and then hearing that basically every survivor, no matter what had happened to us felt that way."

Lisa understood the laughter of audience members as a result of their ability to relate to the material in her bit. She was able to connect with other survivors with similar histories of having their traumas minimized. Lisa transformed the pain of their struggles against rape culture into pleasure "at the idea of disrupting the social order" (Billig 233). Stand-up comedy is one cultural arena in which these connections and pleasures can be generated and affirmed.

Although my emphasis here has, of course, been on the comedic, my goal with this research has never been to discard feelings of sadness or grief. Instead, I aim to recognize, as Patrick Duggan writes, that "there is, it would seem, pleasure in the unpleasurable" (1) and that it is possible and common for us to hold both at once. Trauma affects and implicates the full range of human feelings, and some survivors want to leave their audiences remarking, as Avery hoped his listeners would, "Aw man, that guy's sad... but he killed."

Participants found that opening themselves up to exchanges with other survivors in spaces that centred their comfort was transformative, both in terms of affecting how they defined their own experiences of violence and raising awareness about the ubiquity of sexual violence in their communities and across Canada. Jokes that compel us to hold two or more disparate ideas in our minds at once open possibilities for empathy, critical self-reflection, and the transmission of new information and opinions. But, of course, it is not the duty of the marginalized to educate their oppressors on how to avoid causing further harm; survivors' jokes have intrinsic value beyond their capacity to present an entertaining rebuke to rape culture. Comedy by and for survivors helps us gain footholds in our pain and offers new visions of a future for ourselves— not beyond trauma, per se, but somewhere other than within the dingy doldrums it had been previously assumed we would be held eternally captive.

Works Cited

Billig, Michael. *Laughter and Ridicule: Towards a Social Critique of Laughter.* Sage, 2005.

Brison, Susan. *Aftermath: Violence and the Remaking of a Self.* Princeton University Press, 2003.

Brison, Susan. "Everyday Atrocities and Ordinary Miracles, Or Why I (Still) Bear Witness to Sexual Violence (but Not Too Often)." *Women's Studies Quarterly,* vol. 36, no. 1-2, 2008, pp. 188-98.

Cvetkovich, Ann. *An Archive of Feelings: Trauma, Sexuality, and Lesbian Public Cultures.* Duke University Press, 2003.

Duggan, Patrick. *Trauma-Tragedy: Symptoms of Contemporary Performance.* Manchester University Press, 2012.

Fahs, Breanne. "Naming Sexual Trauma: On the Political Necessity of Nuance in Rape and Sex Offender Discourses." *Critical Trauma Studies: Understanding Violence, Conflict, and Memory in Everyday Life,* edited by Monica J. Casper and Eric Wertheimer, New York University Press, 2016, pp. 61-77.

Frey, Anna. *Who's Laughing Now? Survivors of Sexual Violence Joke about Rape.* 2017, Ryerson University, York University, Master's Thesis.

Herman, Judith Lewis. *Trauma and Recovery.* HarperCollins, 1992.

Jackson, Debra. "Answering the Call: Crisis Intervention and Rape Survivor Advocacy as Witnessing Trauma." *Critical Trauma Studies: Understanding Violence, Conflict, and Memory in Everyday Life,* edited by Monica J. Casper and Eric Wertheimer, New York University Press, 2016, pp. 205-26.

Kahnweiler, Jessie. "Meet My Rapist." *YouTube,* uploaded by Jessie Kahnweiler, 16 Sept. 2013, www.youtube.com/watch?v=_bAAP kqn8Q0. Accessed 26 Dec. 2020.

Lockwood, Patricia. "Rape Joke." *The Awl*, 25 Jul. 2013, www.theawl. com/patricia-lockwood-rape-joke-2e9bd41d80b1#.jzjw3528t. Accessed 26 Dec. 2020.

Meyer, John C. "Humour as a Double Edged Sword: Four Functions of Humour in Communication." *Communication Theory*, vol. 10, no. 3, 2000, pp. 310-31.

Projansky, Sarah. *Watching Rape: Film and Television in Postfeminist Culture.* New York University Press, 2001.

Stevens, Maurice E. "Trauma Is as Trauma Does: The Politics of Affect in Catastrophic Times." *Critical Trauma Studies: Understanding Violence, Conflict, and Memory in Everyday Life*, edited by Monica J. Casper and Eric Wertheimer, New York University Press, 2016, pp. 19-36.

Williams, Raymond. *Marxism and Literature.* Oxford University Press, 1977.

Chapter Five

The *Bad Mothers Club*: In Cyberspace, You Can Hear the Unruly Women Laughing

Anitra Goriss-Hunter

Introduction

Despite feminist interventions, it is obvious that there are serious problems with the ways in which maternal bodies are described and defined. Representations of good and bad mothers offer narrow, restrictive, and prescriptive scripts for maternal bodies. Searching for some possible solutions to the issues concerning restrictive representations of maternity, I found the maternity website, *Bad Mothers Club* (BMC). BMC is a British website, edited and published by Stephanie Calman, that was set up in response to the increasing volume of information about pregnancy and childrearing from a variety of domains, which arguably seek to regulate, control, and profit from maternal bodies. Calman writes that the online publication of *BMC* was "a reaction to the avalanche of advice and criticism a woman is subjected to when she becomes pregnant" as she switches from "being viewed as an intelligent, humorous, thinking person into a fool and a pod" (*BMC*). I argue that *BMC*'s humorous critiques of traditional motherhood draw on a feminist sensibility that underlines the gendered politics of mothering practices in the West and refutes tired, old tropes of maternity. To consider *BMC* as a text in which comic writing enables the delineation and critique of social, cultural, and political norms, I turn to feminist theorists, Nancy Walker, Regina Barrecca, Joanne Gilbert, and Helga Kotthoff. In this chapter, I use the terms "humour" and "comedy" interchangeably.

BMC, however, is not a feminist utopia that continually punctures dominant discourses of mothering. Among moments of feminist subversion, *BMC* also creates narratives that, in unintended ways, support the very images of conventional motherhood that the maternity website lampoons. In order to examine these opposing discourses of subversion and tradition, it is useful to look at what Kathleen Rowe and Angela Stukator refer to as a figure of paradox and excess: "the unruly woman." Although the Bad Mothers, at times, both reinforce and subvert narratives of conventional mothering, their interactive stories have created a fresh type of collective online maternal presence—a self-consciously bad maternity.

Methodology

To examine the ways in which *BMC* paradoxically both supports and challenges conventional representations of maternity, I use four methods. First, I use a feminist lens of critical investigation of the electronic texts. I also employ two forms of textual analysis—discourse analysis and semiotic analysis—to examine the epistemological and ontological meanings that are generated by and cohere to the maternity site. In my investigation of the *BMC*, I examine the ways in which maternal bodies are constructed in cyber(cultural)space by considering whose stories are foregrounded and validated and whose narratives are trivialized and dismissed. The fourth method I use draws upon Christine Hine's notion of "virtual ethnography"—that is, sustained involvement with and analysis of online interactions and the meanings generated from them (8-10, 63-80). My approach differs from general ethnographic methodology, as I select a range of examples and use some retrospective material from website archives.

From 1999 to 2004, I regularly investigated and interacted with the *BMC*, logging on daily to the website. Due to time constraints, from 2004 to 2016 my engagement with the maternity website was reduced to monthly interactions. I want to clearly state my personal investment in the *BMC* because although I explore the site's dark and insightful humour and the ways in which it is mobilized, I also aim to critically investigate the website and give a nuanced rather than partial account of it. Therefore, I focus my critical investigation on the elements of the *BMC* that I argue both challenge and reinstate traditional tropes of motherhood.

The *BMC*

Traditionally, maternal bodies are constructed as variations of the good mother or the bad mother. The conventional good mother is depicted as staying at home to look after the health, wellbeing, and education of her children. She is sometimes represented as frumpy but always ordinary, down to earth, domestic, completely knowable, and dependable—rather like a valued kitchen appliance. She is queen of innumerable advertising campaigns promoting domestic products, such as dishwashing and laundry liquid, whitegoods, food items, and household appliances.

The *BMC*, however, wields wit, satire, and self-conscious observations in order to puncture these fantasies of "good motherhood." The *BMC*'s humorous authoring of mothering narratives, as well as its reclamation of maternal voice and subjectivity and its witty play with conventional notions of maternity, are aptly summed up in the site's title, tagline, and accompanying graphic. This club, which invites other mothers to join, self-consciously describes its members as bad mothers, who define themselves in opposition to the traditional good mother. The name of the group—the Bad Mothers Club—encapsulates the Bad Mothers' humorous reworking, rejection, and ridicule of the impossibly exacting standards of contemporary maternity, as espoused by a range of print, film, online, and digital maternity texts. This rejection through humour radiates from the name of the group to its accompanying graphic. In contrast to the smiling or serene mothers and babies that illustrate most mainstream maternity websites, the image placed alongside the *BMC* title is that of a martini glass. Tilted on an angle, the glass is filled with clear fluid, and perched on the rim is a child's pacifier, taking the place of a cocktail garnish. A purple handle on the pacifier is reflected in the purple print that proclaims "Bad Mothers Club." The *BMC* slogan under this heading states that "In the aisle by the chill cabinets, no-one can hear you scream." This line enacts a playful reworking of the advertising tagline from the 1979 film, *Alien*: "In space no one can hear you scream." *Alien* is a science-fiction thriller, in which a spaceship (nicknamed

"Mother"), on a mission into outer space, is invaded by aliens, who incubate inside and then burst out of human bodies. The *BMC*'s refashioning of the original line draws on a well-known moment of popular culture to humorously align maternity and domesticity with monstrosity and horror. The Bad Mothers of *BMC* construct themselves as monstrous and grotesque but also hilarious. As the founder and editor of *BMC*, Stephanie Calman presents herself as the Bad Mother par excellence, as her witty and insightful writings reflect upon how contemporary motherhood is constructed and represented as conventional in various media.

Humour

The notion of "humour" is difficult to define, as there is always a strongly subjective element to its interpretation. I describe it as text in a particular context that is coded and/or perceived as amusing and/or funny. Although the subject matter of humour is limitless, women have historically often been the butt of jokes (Willett et al. 217), representing "to-be-laughed-at-ness" (Gilbert 324). According to Gilbert, such objectification of women is fuelled by the "male guffaw" (156, 163)— an extension of Laura Mulvey's (14-38) concept of the "male gaze."

The ways in which humour has been used to refuse restrictive conventions of gender and femininity have been well documented (Barreca; Gilbert; Weaver, Mora, and Morgan). Moreover, much has been written about the forms of comedic subversion often used by women, which range from self-deprecatory humour to comic performances of marginality and cultural criticism in the form of jokes. However, these accounts offer only a partial discussion of the humorous comments and critique that specifically relate to contemporary maternity. The Bad Mothers of the *BMC* swagger into the gap in this research and offer humorous explorations of issues relevant to maternal bodies in the twenty-first century.

Gleefully flouting the exhortations of the good mother to be domestic, patient, acquiescent, and quiet, the Bad Mothers of *BMC* express their anger at the restrictions that conventional motherhood seeks to impose on maternal bodies. In this chapter, I argue that the Bad Mothers use humour and ridicule as a means of critiquing dominant representations of gender and maternity. This mobilization of humour and ridicule subverts the conventional use of these elements as disciplinary techniques that produce gender hegemony (Billig 5, 201-02) and a gendered humour that creates "self-regulating subjects" (Abedinifard 234). The Bad Mothers make use of the central role of gendered humour to extend the types of women's (and, at times, feminist) humour expressed throughout the website to include bad maternity. I explore how these Bad Mothers subvert traditional tropes of motherhood by using humour to claim subjectivity, author their own stories of self and maternity, and critique conventional mothering ideas and practices.

In contrast to more mainstream mothering sites, *BMC* relies upon a humorous approach to the topic of maternity. It is possible to enjoy reading the *BMC* solely as an extremely funny text. *BMC* also, on one level, identifies, outlines, and renders humorous the gendered inconsistencies inherent in narratives of contemporary motherhood and ensures that the website is potentially a potent source of subversion of dominant discourses of maternity.

The humour-saturated writings of the Bad Mothers on the *BMC* site overcome what Kotthoff (5, 13-21) terms the "double marginalization" of women engaging in humorous speech (see also Bilger; Barreca; Levy). Although women continue to be marginalized in the area of comic expression, female writers and performers who rely on humorous narratives in their work possess the potential to overturn conventional notions of gender and humour (Walker; Crawford; Kotthoff; Gadd). I argue that *BMC* extends into cyber(cultural)space Walker's notion that women's humour is a means of overcoming conventional representations of females as passive and subordinate to dominant male culture.

As the authors of and audience for their own humorous maternity narratives, the Bad Mothers of the *BMC* subvert the objectification of women as the butt of jokes and humorous stories. The agency of this kind of bad maternity mobilizes humour and anger in order to overturn the "male guffaw" and replace it with examples of what I term the "maternal guffaw"—a version of an empowered maternal gaze situated in humorous comments and jokes as well as in the reception of these utterances. Bad Mothers make humorous and insightful comments that reveal and puncture restrictive narratives of traditional motherhood. They self-consciously set up themselves and motherhood in general as the butt of the joke and then laugh long and loudly at their own subversive and funny stories and comments.

Unruly Women

In order to investigate the ways in which the Bad Mothers' use of humour paradoxically both subverts and embraces traditional narratives of maternity, I draw upon the notion of the "unruly woman" (Rowe; Stukator), who stands beyond boundaries of the normative. As with stand-up comics, those who create and perform humorous material are briefly able to step outside the bounds of conventional behaviours and norms in order to produce humorous moments (Russell). Such temporary permission to reject the restrictions of dominant discourse is important for women, as it permits them to tell and examine their own narratives, which are often ignored or trivialized by mainstream culture, without alienating a potentially diverse audience. Historically, women's humorous transgressions of convention can be expressed as behaviours associated with the unruly woman (Rowe; Stukator). This transgressive woman embodies Bakhtin's notion of "carnival" in her humorous exchanges that challenge traditional conceptions of femininity. The unruly woman is a laughing figure of excess who "often enjoys a reprieve from those fates that so often seem inevitable to women under patriarchy, because her home is comedy and the carnivalesque, the realm of inversion and fantasy where, for a time at least, the ordinary world can be stood on its head" (Rowe 11). Unruly female bodies are associated with grotesqueness, dirt, and liminality. These attributes come together in the figure of the maternal body, "which, through menstruation, pregnancy, childbirth, and lactation, participates uniquely in the carnivalesque drama of 'becoming,' of inside-out and outside-in, death-in-life and life-in-death" (Rowe 33-34).

The Bad Mothers mobilize the carnivalesque and inversion for their own purposes. They make fun of the conventions of motherhood, ridiculing traditional tropes and rendering them as carnivalized and inverted in their own narratives. Calman and the other contributors to *BMC* construct a Bad Mother persona by taking the negative stereotype of the vocal, fleshy, pleasure-seeking, non-domestic, and middle-class housewife and render that cliché as a funny and positive narrative.

Just as these Bad Mothers invert and carnivalize traditional tropes of motherhood, they also refuse to accept the conventional suppression of women's anger directed at normative discourses. Rowe claims that women's anger is culturally perceived to be objectionable and that it is undertheorized in feminist film and cultural studies. Traditional tropes of femininity and maternity are unable to articulate anger and rage. This is where the Bad Mothers of *BMC*, who are not good mothers or "nice girls," are able to laughingly express their anger at the inequities and restrictions inherent in the strict boundaries that conventional motherhood delineates and polices. Although the Bad Mothers of the *BMC* focus on such topics as motherhood, children, housework, men and beauty, which are the usual topics dealt with by "domestic humourists," like Erma Bombeck (Rowe 69-70, 134), the former articulate their dissatisfaction with idealized depictions of traditional motherhood with angry and tough feminist jokes, ridicule, and laughter which are well received in the *BMC* community.

Unlike the "domestic humourists" (Rowe 69-70, 134) who support a conventional take on maternity, the Bad Mothers of *BMC* mobilize a humorous critique of traditional tropes of maternity, which is similar to the unruly constructions of maternity performed by a number of contemporary fictional television mothers. In her analysis of television mothers in such shows as *AbFab*, *Sex in the City*, and *X-Files*, Terrie Waddell writes that "Fictional television 'mums' have become speaking (often loud, unruly and vulgar) subjects who contribute to the redefining of mother as anything *but* selfless, passive and bound to the maternal" (182). In contrast to the televisual representations of unruly mothering, the Bad Mothers author their own stories, freely vent their anger, and using the qualities of cyber(cultural)space, collectively construct a bad maternity.

In contrast to other individual humorous representations of mothering, the Bad Mothers offer collective funny critiques of traditional tropes of motherhood. In the *BMC* forums, individual voices add their own tales that are usually received with positive feedback and similar stories to support the initial posting. These narratives create ongoing stories and metanarratives of bad maternity. The threads of story in these strands connect with one another through expressions of the "maternal guffaw" that laugh through the tales.

The unruly woman also suggests different ways of thinking about power and the politics of looking, which may involve "the female gaze" (Taylor 397-400) and the means to alter how female images are viewed. Rowe argues that "Because public power is predicated largely on visibility, men have long understood the need to secure their power not only by looking but by being seen, or rather, by fashioning—as subject, as author, as artist—a spectacle of themselves" (11). The participants of the *BMC* seem to enjoy constructing themselves as humorous spectacle and creating a fresh maternal subjectivity of Bad Mothers, who revel in a cocktail of pithy narratives, anger, and laughter at traditional tropes of motherhood.

Even though the unruly woman expresses her defiance of social and cultural norms, paradoxically, she also supports traditional concepts and classifications. The impermanence of the transgressive carnival, in which inversion is righted, eventually reestablishes conventional political and social order. Peter Stallybrass and Allon White claim the "most politically thoughtful commentators wonder ... whether the 'licensed release' of carnival is not simply a form of social control of the low by the high and therefore serves the interest of that very official culture which it apparently opposes" (13). The unruly woman's challenges to convention, therefore, both subvert and uphold norms as they are built upon paradox (Stukator 199-212).

Bad vs. Good—Unruly Bad Mothers

Bad Mother bodies proclaim themselves to be excessive and unruly throughout the website. For example, in the merchandise section of the website, an advertisement for a *BMC* tote bag emblazoned with the slogan "I am an old bag" features a somewhat dishevelled, plus-sized, mature-age model. This unruly woman, representing the Bad Mothers, stares defiantly at the viewer. The graphic depicts the excess, mature flesh of a woman, who appears to be both aware of her status as a Bad Mother and enjoys the humour of the situation.

The Bad Mothers' humorous self-authored critique of images of conventional maternity is enabled and promoted by the qualities and capabilities of cyber(cultural)space. Although Calman and her writings are a feature of the website, the *BMC* is written by a number of guest authors and forum participants. In contrast to the more mainstream maternity websites, *BMC* refuses to accept the binaries of author/reader and appropriate/deviant maternal as Bad Mothers write their own narratives that do not fit within conventional stories of motherhood. Discussion threads usually attract a number of postings that add different stories or elements of story to form a multilayered narrative. *BMC* is created through interconnected ideas and tales written by the Bad

Mothers and linked, literally at times, throughout the website.

Throughout *BMC*, Calman and the other Bad Mothers tell tales of how they refuse the role of the good mother by, for instance, presenting their families with easy fast-food instead of nutritionally sound meals, throwing out extremely dirty clothes rather than washing them, and telling their children the facts of life in such a way that the children become frightened and disgusted rather than relieved at receiving accurate information concerning sexual behaviour and reproduction. The inversions within these carnivalesque tales foreground the unruly rejections of convention that are gleefully performed by the Bad Mothers.

Calman revels in her persona as Bad Mother extraordinaire, and she constantly mobilizes humour to comment upon contemporary versions of the good mother. For instance, in an example of Calman's deflating of maternal norms, she writes: "Term is due to start again: phew. Worn out through the holidays by running alongside the children while they rollerblade—their new craze, Peter and I were by the second week begging them to watch more TV" (*BMC*). Calman's humorous inversion writes back to the plethora of articles in mainstream print and online magazines that prescribe numerous extracurricular activities and domestic duties to be undertaken by the contemporary good mother. Watching television is not one of these activities.

While the predominantly cheerful tone of most commercial maternity websites reinforces notions of the good mother, the *BMC* espouses angry, dark humour, which enables the Bad Mothers to assume positions of power by critiquing traditional discourses of maternity. For instance, the posts on the *BMC* forums usually contradict the upbeat tone and positive subject matter of the mainstream maternity sites in messages such as "crap week coming up, why are my kids such a nightmare" (*BMC*). Other posts in this thread sympathize with the mother complaining about her children, thus forming a group narrative of bad maternity on this topic. When a *BMC* discussion thread began asking for ideas to keep children occupied during wet winter weather, one Bad Mother jokingly suggested "drugging them." Another thread enquired about "cleaning tips" to prepare a house for sale. The advice offered by Bad Mothers included the following: "Dull piano keys? Wash with alcohol on a one for you and one for me basis."

In striking contrast to the lightly humorous tone of conventional maternity websites, the humour of the *BMC* liberally draws on undertones and outward expressions of anger. This anger is most apparent when discussion threads explore issues related to a gendered division of labour in the home or when traditional notions of marriage are investigated. Bad Mothers often comment that, in their opinion, their husbands/ partners do not do their share of housework. This issue is often summed up by Bad Mothers stating that their husbands/partners are incapable of multitasking: they fail to do more than one household task at a time and that is usually done in a begrudging manner. For instance, in a thread discussing this issue, one Bad Mother stated with undertones of anger that her husband could multitask a bit: "He can game and watch tv at the same time" (BMC). The stereotype of blissful heterosexual marriage is deflated in posts in which Bad Mothers express anger and disillusionment with their partners. In these instances, humour and ridicule are not used to maintain gender hegemony; instead, they are employed to puncture dominant discourses. A humorous example of this puncturing occurred in a post with the title "stupid chefboy is limping around all pathetic and wanting sympathy" (BMC). Another Bad Mother responded to this message by stating "Tell him he'll find SYMPATHY in the dictionary ... between shit and syphilis!!" (BMC). One of the BMC topic threads that dealt with a range of issues concerning household labour and partner support was titled "F*ck, Sh*t, Bo*llocks!" These are just a few examples of how the Bad Mothers use anger, humour, and ridicule to collectively author narratives that write back to ostensibly happy traditional tropes of motherhood. The cuttingly humorous threads written by the Bad Mothers stand in sharp contrast to the cheerfully sympathetic messages of the contributors to mainstream and commercial maternity site forums.

In the writings of the Bad Mothers, however, the good mother and her attachment to conventional maternity haunts the text. To further examine these threads of bad haunted by good maternity, I turn again to the notion of the unruly woman (Rowe; Stukator). Bad Mothers are unruly mothers who refuse but also support traditional tropes of maternity. For instance, in contrast to the slender, well-groomed, and happy mothers and the immaculate, cheerful children on the mainstream maternity sites, the accompanying graphic for Calman's regular feature is a photograph of the editor looking frazzled while her infant son screams in her arms. Although only the upper part of Calman's body is visible, it is obvious that she is the opposite of the slim, smiling, and blonde mothers, who are typically depicted on mainstream sites dealing capably with their docile infants or children. Calman's fleshiness, wind-blown dark hair, and awkward position—as she grapples with a screaming baby attempting to wriggle out of her grasp—embody the unruly mother. The positioning of this image at the beginning of a column that laughs at but also acknowledges personal and societal yearnings to fulfil the stereotype of conventionally attractive maternal bodies places Calman in a position of paradox: she is a subversive unruly mother but is also defined by traditional tropes of maternity. Although Calman strongly critiques normative maternity and gender stereotypes in her regular column, she also embraces dominant narratives of maternal bodies in her expressed longings for a more conventionally attractive appearance, well-behaved children, and greater abilities in performing domestic tasks. In these examples, Calman's articles about social and cultural expectations of maternal bodies and her writing back to these ideas form a polysemic expression that both reinforces conventional discourses of motherhood and also creates space for the subversion of dominant narratives of maternity.

In a polysemic expression, Calman's work sums up the ambivalence, paradox, and excess of the unruly mother. Many examples of the unruly mother surface in Calman's writings for *BMC*. She regularly writes articles that set the subversive tone of the site and give editorial authority to the rejection of traditional images of maternity. Calman's pieces focus on her own family life and the ways in which she refuses to shape some of her views and experiences according to normative expectations of Western, middle-class maternity, which are frequently alluded to in mainstream texts. As these writings are shaped for an audience, the boundaries between fiction and lived experience are blurred. Calman's articles are chatty and funny; she writes back to the evacuation of maternal subjectivity in favour of maternal obedience and containment within strict culturally determined limits of a bourgeois maternity. However, her written longings to have a slimmer body, better behaved children, and a more domestically organized home life also indicate a desire for the conventional ideal of maternity that she scorns as a Bad Mother. These ambivalent shiftings produce a paradox and polysemic expression in which the unruly mother both challenges and supports conventional notions of maternity. Although the Bad Mothers of *BMC* reinscribe conventional maternity in terms of longing for some of the trappings of traditional middle-class motherhood, they also use acerbic humour and ridicule to challenge other normative discourses of mothering. Collectively, they refute traditional narratives of motherhood that attempt to contain maternal bodies within the domestic sphere and render mothers subservient to the perceived needs of their family. It is precisely the image espoused by the good mothers of maternal bodies as perpetually vigilant child producers, carers, wives, consumers, and products themselves that provides an easy target for the angry humour of the Bad Mothers.

The *BMC* celebrates the recasting of conventional maternal bodies (good mothers) as autonomous, intelligent women who struggle to fulfil their own desires. The website sets out to lampoon the traditional maternity that casts those who identify with the images of mothers on the mainstream maternity webpages as good mothers and that reduces all those outside their sphere to the position of Bad Mother. In a project of reclamation, the *BMC* collectively constructs their maternal bodies as being awash in a(n) (alcoholic) cocktail of desire, anger, pleasure, commerce, popular culture, technology, and self-authored maternity narratives.

Conclusion

In conclusion, the *BMC* creates a polysemic expression that supports conventional motherhood but also creates many possibilities to challenge the discourses of traditional maternity, which still infest hard copy and electronic texts. On the one hand, the website satirizes conventional constructions of motherhood in ways that are ambivalent and, in doing so, reinstates these discourses of traditional maternity. Implicit in the writings on the website are narratives in which the Bad Mothers' yearnings surface for the trappings of a conventional middle-class British maternity: domestic, coupled, heterosexual, white, and, self-sacrificing, with well-behaved, talented children and a successful part-time career.

However, the *BMC* also opens up (cyber)space in which maternal voices are asserted and heard. The website cleverly uses angry, dark humour as well as ridicule to puncture dominant discourses of motherhood. As unruly women, these mothers celebrate the ways in which they exceed the Western model of ideal maternity: they are fleshy, loud, angry at times, and they enjoy drinking alcohol and laughing with their female friends. The Bad Mothers humorously celebrate being slothful, disasters in the kitchen, and unable to sew costumes. They delight in poking fun at the whole institution of motherhood. While the good mothers look out smilingly from their print and electronic texts—upholding a contemporary and commercialized version of the 1950's housewife—the Bad Mothers' funny stories and unruly behaviour enable the development of an empowered maternal gaze and "maternal guffaw" through the authoring of their own humorous mother stories, the reclamation of expressions of anger, and the collective construction of (bad) maternal subjectivities.

Works Cited

Abedinifard, Mostafa. "Ridicule, Gender Hegemony, and the Disciplinary Function of Mainstream Gender Humour." *Social Semiotics*, vol. 26, no. 3, 2016, pp. 234-49.

Alien. Directed by Ridley Scott, Twentieth Century Fox, 1979.

Bakhtin, Mikhail. *Rabelais and His World*. Translated by Helene Iswolsky. Indiana University Press, 1984.

Barreca, Regina., editor. *Last Laughs: Perspectives on Women and Comedy. Studies in Gender and Culture*. Volume 2, Gordon and Breach, 1988.

Barreca, Regina. *They Used to call me Snow White ... but I Drifted: Women's Strategic Use of Humour*. Penguin, 1992.

Bilger, Audrey. *Laughing Feminism: Subversive Comedy in Frances Burney, Maria Edgeworth, and Jane Austen*. Wayne State University Press, 1998.

Billig, Michael. *Laughter and Ridicule: Towards a Social Critique of Humour*. Sage Publications, 2005.

Bombeck, Erma. *The Best of Bombeck: A Treasury of Works by America's Favorite Humourist*. Galahad Books, 1993.

Calman, Stephanie. *Bad Mothers Club*. 2003, www.badmothersclub.co.uk. Accessed 27 Dec. 2020.

Crawford, Mary. "Gender and Humour in Social Context." *Journal of Pragmatics*, vol. 35, no. 9, 2003, pp. 1413-30.

Gilbert, Joanne R. *Performing Marginality: Humour, Gender and Cultural Critique*. Wayne State University Press, 2004.

Hine, Christine. *Virtual Ethnography.* Sage Publications, Ltd, 2000.

Kotthoff, Helga. "Gender and Humour: The State of the Art." *Journal of Pragmatics*, vol. 38, 2006, pp. 4-25.

Levy, Barbara. *Ladies Laughing: Wit as Control in Contemporary Women Writers.* Routledge, 1997.

Mulvey, Laura. *Visual and Other Pleasures.* Indiana University Press, 1989.

Rowe, Kathleen. *The Unruly Woman: Gender and the Genres of Laughter.* The University of Texas Press, 1995.

Russell, Danielle. "Self-Deprecatory Humour and the Female Comic: Self- Destruction or Comedic Construction?" *Thirdspace*, vol. 2, no. 1, 2002, thirdspace.ca/articles/druss.htm. Accessed 27 Dec. 2020.

Stallybrass, Peter, and Allon White. *The Politics and Poetics of Transgression.* Methuen, 1986.

Stukator, Angela. "It's Not Over Until the Fat Lady Sings: Comedy, the Carnivalesque, and the Body Politics." *Bodies Out of Bounds: Fatness and Transgression*, edited by Jana Evans Braziel and Kathleen LeBesco, University of California Press, 2001, pp. 197-212.

Suleiman, Susan Rubin. "Writing and Motherhood." *The (M)other Tongue: Essays in Feminist Psychoanalytic Interpretation*, edited by Shirley Nelson Garner, Claire Kahane, and Madelon Sprengnether, Cornell University Press, 1985, pp. 352-77.

Taylor, Jessica. "Romance and the Female Gaze Obscuring Gendered Violence in The Twilight Saga." *Feminist Media Studies*, vol, 14, no. 3, 2014, pp. 388-402.

Waddell, Terrie. *Mis/takes: Archetypes, Myth and Identity in Screen Fiction.* Routledge, 2006.

Weaver, Simon, Raul A. Mora, and Karen Morgan. "Gender and Humour: Examining Discourses of Hegemony and Resistance." *Social Semiotics*, vol. 26, no. 3, 2016, pp. 227-33.

Walker, Nancy. A. *A Very Serious Thing: Women's Humour and American Culture.* University of Minnesota, 1988.

Willett, Cynthia, Julie Willett, and Yael D Sherman. "The Seriously Erotic Politics of Feminist Laughter." *Social Research—Politics and Comedy*, vol. 79, no. 1, 2012, pp. 217-46.

Chapter Six

Making It Up As They Go Along: An Analysis of Feminist Comedy in the Prairies

Marley Duckett

It is early evening in Saskatoon; September is just a few days old, and the weather is still warm for Saskatchewan at this time of year. The sleepy brick buildings on Broadway Theatre are painted in the glow of a soon-to-be setting sun, and traffic is light. People amble down the street holding cups of coffee in their hands. I hear glasses clinking on the dreamy Una patio and swerve through strikingly beautiful hipsters smoking outside of the Broadway Theatre. As I pass Calories, the dessert shop, I glance with longing at delicate tables laden with cheesecake and tea, and I tell myself to order some nachos when I get to Amigos Cantina. Everyone is dressed in shorts and t-shirts, summer dresses, and flipflops; we remain united in collective defiance of impending autumn winds, which, every year, seem to visit the city too early. I am in a hurry. The ping of my phone spurs my pace—ping, ping, ping! Likely, Jenny, my castmate, is texting us to say that she is at the venue, that she went inside, that she made it to the back room, that she is going to order food, that she is tired, that she is excited to see us, and that we need to hurry and set up the chairs. After a brief pause, my phone sounds again. That will be Courtney telling us she will be late. I smile to myself; these texts have become ceremonial, a necessary ritual to set the tone for every single improv show we perform together. Jenny

Ryan, Courtney Lato, and I make up the trio that is LadyBits Improv Comedy Collective.

Women are still a recognized minority within comedy performers (Smith). This certainly remains true in Canada's prairie provinces. It is not uncommon to attend live comedic theatre in Saskatoon and find it heavily dominated by male performers. By comedic theatre, I am referring to improv, stand-up, and sketch. We founded LadyBits Improv Comedy Collective after recognizing the under- and misrepresentation of women in the Saskatoon comedy scene. LadyBits is Saskatchewan's first all-female professional improv team, and we focus on creating safe spaces for female and female-identified people to develop skills and to create performance opportunities for comedic actors at any skill level. Our stage has served members of the LGBTQ+ community, Indigenous women, and people of colour, and it has also been described as "a place to go because you don't fit in anywhere else," which has become a sort of anthem fuelling our work. We asked questions about women and comedy in Saskatoon. Do women desire to participate in the existing comedy spaces in Saskatoon? If so, then why are there so few women performing in these spaces? How can we explain the lack of female representation on stages in the comedy culture of Saskatoon? Throughout this chapter, I will use the formation of LadyBits Improv Comedy Collective as an example to illustrate the rise of feminist comedy in the prairie provinces.

To understand the impact that LadyBits has had on the comedy scene in Saskatoon, it is important to first illustrate the history of improv in this city. I came to Saskatoon, a wee babe of a student, at seventeen years old. I began my undergraduate degrees at the University of Saskatchewan, and it was in one of those first-year classes that a fellow student announced a call for improvisers looking to perform on a local improv team. Having already studied improv for four years, at a competitive level, I jumped at the opportunity to audition for a professional team. What struck me was that I was answering a call for a gender-specific role—"We need girls, so please ladies, think about auditioning!" When I later auditioned and made the team, I thought about this more critically. Did I make the team because of my training and skill (if there was such a thing as being a classically trained improviser, I was it), or did I make the team because my biological hardware filled a gap I was just beginning to realize was there? Furthermore, should I have been angry about this, or should I have been happy to see some degree of equal gender representation on stages?

Long before I entered the comedy scene, Saskatoon had two major professional comedic improv teams: The Saskatoon Soaps, founded in 1983, and The Flying Fish Fun Factory, founded in 1995. If only I had the word count to regale you with tales of hazing, competition, and showmanship that occurred between these two teams, but believe me when I say that after some serious downsizing and structural changes, The Flying Fish Fun Factory rebranded and became the beloved local troupe known as The No-No's Comedy Group. Since its creation, the LadyBits has become a major player in the improv scene, and in addition to the Saskatoon Soaps, The No-No's, the university team, and other smaller groups performing occasionally, improv in Saskatoon is thriving.

Jenny and I met and got to know each other while working with the No-No's, and Courtney had a long-standing contract with the Soaps. Collectively, the three of us have over thirty years of improv experience. After reaching out to Courtney, Jenny approached me and asked me what I thought about the lack of strong female representation in the comedy scene and if I would be interested in starting something new and different. At the time, local teams consisted of ten actors or more, with a mixed-cast and short-form performance style. There were no self-identified feminist troupes and certainly no all-female troupes working in the city. There were other women interested in joining the troupe, but, ultimately, schedules, time restraints, and divergent performance expectations fashioned the trio LadyBits would become. I was intrigued at the idea of working with new people and to explore this word "feminism" I had heard so much about. I decided to join Jenny and Courtney. We named the troupe LadyBits in homage to our all-female cast, with "bits" referring to comedic bits, or sections of a comedy routine. We intended the name to not only salute women in comedy but to also refer to comedic materials created and performed by funny women. The double entendre was just for fun. We knew we had chosen a good name when we received complaints from an anonymous caller, stating the name was distasteful and shameful for women everywhere. "You might as well call yourselves The Vaginas!" said the caller and abruptly hung up the phone. We encountered barriers before we had even begun. Jenny once said something along the lines of, "If we want LadyBits to be successful, we must promise to hustle a little bit, every single day." She meant that LadyBits would have to work hard to succeed in a town where comedy still meant othering minorities, making rape jokes at the expense of the victim, and eating generous servings of patriarchy pie. We kept that promise throughout our first year as a troupe. While maintaining a regular rehearsal and workshop schedule, we also worked with freelance consultant Jeanine Fahlman to help us establish a brand. We devised a logo, slogan, and artistic look. We created business cards, handbills, posters, and social media accounts. We set in motion a plan to establish ourselves as bona fide comedic performers. We defined our improv philosophy and affirmed our goals—we are a troupe dedicated to creating safe spaces and performance opportunities for women to try their hand at comedy.

We had such phenomenally grand plans, as well as tragically ironic plans, that I can't believe I didn't laugh harder when we completely tanked during those first few months. We were going to rally together our performers, our male supporters, and our feminist actors and comedians. We were going to break open the seal of injustice and reclaim the stage that had eluded us for so long. We were going to make a serious change in the comedy scene in the prairies. So, imagine our surprise when the strongest reaction our new new-wave feminist troupe received was indifference. I recall a moderately successful local comedian assuring us that he just knew we would not make it past the first year. Sure, we had a few people who told us what a great idea it was, a few who thought it was ridiculous and unnecessary, and a few more who didn't get it. But, mostly, nobody cared. Reflecting on it now, I think that this reaction carried significant weight and had a profound effect on our identity as a troupe. Peers ignoring our articulated and identified concerns fuelled a desire to bring feminist theory to the forefront of the collective comedy conscience.

As with most grassroots projects, LadyBits fumbled and stumbled our way through the first year of performances. We started a few projects; some worked, and some didn't. We briefly partnered with The Broadway Theatre on a project in which we led feminist critiques of movie hits. We dedicated our Sunday afternoons to debating the legitimacy of the Bechdel test; we argued the power of pagan feminism and critiqued Alicia Silverstone's famous satirical performance of Emma in *Clueless*. We were boring but wonderful, and slowly people stopped attending, perhaps because feminist film critique just wasn't as entertaining as losing oneself in the easiness of comedic film. We also advertised joke-making seminars, which were underattended, and offered corporate training using improvisational technique, but no one called us. We reached out to fellow comedians and improvisers, asking for advice and support, but we were met with disinterest and, in some cases, even resistance. In one example, a fellow female improvisor who we had worked with for a few years dodged our calls and ignored our emails. Much later, and after some coaxing, this improvisor admitted she thought we were going to bully her into caring about feminism; she described the whole thing as "intense." I guess we were intense; we had set out to unite the women working in the comedy scene only to realize that we were the women working in the comedy scene. We were wrangling a nonexistent group of people, which forced us to rethink our approach. Briony Smith was right when she writes "Making it as a non-male comedian requires resilience." LadyBits needed to work harder. We reached out to other performers in the city, not necessarily comedians but actors, directors, writers, and general theatre folk, who were known for working with feminist material and who weren't afraid to address difficult material on their stages.

To succeed in those circles, LadyBits became multifaceted. Whereas once we were focused on improv, we decided to incorporate a variety of theatrical disciplines to expand our reach. Jenny began performing in local open-mic nights with stand-up routines deconstructing misogyny, satirizing the challenges of motherhood, and romanticizing postapocalyptic wastelands. Courtney, who we fondly refer to as the "actor" of the group, worked her media connections and got us involved with fundraisers and theatre companies. We have worked with Dress for Success, LadyBall, Fem-Fest, Go With the Flow, Live-Five Theatre, CFCR Radio, and others. I created a lasting partnership with Persephone Theatre, wherein we began teaching annual improv classes for women and started teaching workshops at the University of Saskatchewan. In my professional life, I study anthropology, and as a graduate student, one of my responsibilities is to teach Anthropology 111. In preparation for teaching this course, I became certified in university philosophies of teaching. After discussing the benefits of improv in one of my papers, the instructor for the course asked if I would teach a series of workshops through the Gwenna Moss Centre for Teaching and Learning. My focus was on incorporating improv in the classroom; I taught teachers how to use these skills in their lecture prep and in their teacher-student interaction in order to increase good rapport building between teachers and students. Despite one man insisting that because I was so funny, I should tell jokes about how fat I am (cringe), the workshops ran smoothly. I think I learned more about my own teaching than I was able to teach others, but it was such a wonderful realization that other working professionals could see the value of improv in disciplines existing outside of theatre and entertainment. Unlike other classes in the city, our class blends traditional theatre knowledge and skills with practices specific to comedy, all through a feminist lens. People take our classes for a variety of reasons; some want to learn more about improv, some want to make friends with other comedic performers, and some who were dragged there by a friend wanting to claim the two-for-one deal.

Much of our early work was rooted in the sharing of skills, an assortment of back-scratching exchanges between theatre companies that helped us connect with people outside of the regular comedy scene. One of our first performances was a variety-style showcase featuring an assortment of female comedians. Artistic directors, well-known television and radio personalities, successful actors, local government officials, and playwrights attended. With support from the larger theatre community, word spread about LadyBits and our feminist approach to performance. Almost overnight, LadyBits became well-known in the city; we were performing for local theatre companies as invited guests and headlining events we had never been considered for before. LadyBits has become an avid participant in charity events and benefits. Some of our greatest work has been in support of others succeeding in philanthropic endeavours and effecting seriously positive changes for women in Saskatchewan. Without a doubt, and in various capacities, interest in feminist humour is growing in the prairies; public perspectives regarding what is funny and attitudes towards feminist performers are shifting. I believe the continued support of LadyBits and others like us—including female improvisors from the University of Saskatchewan as well as local comedians now taking their own initiatives to form female comedy troupes and host writing workshops, seminars, and classes—is a testament of this.

Despite a somewhat frantic and chaotic beginning, I accredit LadyBits's failures as fantastic growing pains that helped us build credibility and legitimacy in the improv community in Saskatoon.

Shedding some of our endeavours was the result of an acute focus on our goals, of our approach in performance, and of the development of our niche in the community. Creating more holistic practices added to the authenticity of our presence on comedic stages and infused our performances with the confidence we needed to turn improvisational theatrical skill into good performance practice. We soon drew media attention and started appearing in news and radio interviews, podcasts, blogs, and in the local newspaper. I recall thinking I had made it big when an excited couple stopped me in the street to tell me they had seen me on the news and decided to attend our show. They gushed about how funny we were, how they now come to every performance, and thought our name was very clever. I didn't have the heart, or the ego, to tell them that our name was LadyBits and not LadyParts. (Regardless, move over Second City. The people love us. Just kidding! You are a god among mortals. Please hire us.)

After gaining recognition and success for being a funny improv troupe, people, mostly women, began approaching the troupe collectively to ask us about our personal histories, how to tell jokes, or how to deal with personal traumas using comedic practice. In our early career, LadyBits worked to fix a problem that only seemed to matter to us. However, we now were confronted with a reality we had only previously assumed: Women use comedy to address important social issues.

Creating a comedy community that included women had been a primary objective for LadyBits. When we began to see an increase of feminist comedians and improvisors taking to the comedy stages in Saskatoon, we realized that we had, to some degree, succeeded in creating safer spaces for women (and men) to practice feminist comedy. In the words of a LadyBits student and regular performer, "There was such a diverse group.... We were all very different, but many of us still had the same fears and apprehensions.... Our openness, our vulnerability, and our acceptance of ourselves and each other forged a friendship and a family" (Rothenburger). In addition, what started as focused networking with like-minded individuals blossomed into long-lasting professional relationships. LadyBits felt a social responsibility to share our skills with others who were new to their comedy practice. We have a meaningful relationship with Saskatoon's Persephone Theatre, the largest live theatre house in Saskatchewan. Through Persephone, LadyBits has taught an annual beginner and intermediate improv class for women. Teaching allows for the sharing of knowledge, the critical discussion of feminist practice, and the ability to connect with individuals outside of our regular audience. A student once remarked: "The classroom itself was also a place where walls came down: playful and creative, it was encouraging to see people allow themselves to take risks, to engage and step out of being composed or reserved.... Sincere support provided a unique atmosphere for meeting other women from a variety of generations" (Gooijer). Although LadyBits will always specialize in improv, we wanted to commit to our brand; we are a comedy collective. As such, when Dana Pihach, general manager of O'Brian's Event Centre, contacted us and offered to sponsor a monthly show, we were ecstatic. We worked with O'Brian's for years and loved it. Now, we are at Drift Cafe and Vista Lounge, a beautiful space along the river. In addition to our regular improv shows, LadyBits, with Drift, now produces a monthly comedy open-mic night for female and female-identified performers to try their hand at comedy. The show, aptly titled "#womencrushwednesdays," runs on the second Wednesday of every month and has had a steady increase in attendance as the show grows in popularity. We were honoured when the University of Saskatchewan's student improv team reached out to us; they invited us to teach workshops, to perform in their festivals, and to participate as a godmother, which has revealed itself as something akin to an improv oracle meets a hypegirl. Men and women in various professions, across ages, and with degrees of skill and experience, continue to interact, perform, and support each other. With nearly fourteen years of performing comedic improv in Saskatchewan, I am excited to see new methods, forms, humour, and people represented on stage. It might not have been an articulated objective, but, certainly, redefining comedy in Saskatoon, is an outcome of the work LadyBits has done.

Despite our success working in comedy, LadyBits has received notable backlash and criticism for our work. Anna Fields critiques performances that use gender as a hook to entice audience attendance (Fields xxvi). She warns readers that in advertising shows boasting "women" as the reason to attend, we make the show about acknowledging a token female performer and not necessarily about highlighting funny women for their talent and hard work: "Such implicit, subconscious segregation ('Here we have the women, and here we have the actual "funny people"') forced these groundbreakers ... to make the best of their situation" (xxvi).

Similarly, LadyBits has been accused of implementing the same exclusionary structures that inspired the formation of the troupe in the first place. During our first few months producing "#womencrushwednesdays," a fellow male comedian claimed he would never attend our shows because he knew he wouldn't be able to perform. We were surprised that an event made with the intention to create safe space and performance opportunity would be met with accusations of purposeful and curated exclusion. In another instance, a stand-up comedian articulated disdain for our show's structure, claiming that we should let in other comedians for free as a professional courtesy. In stand-up culture, free entrance is a sign of respect; many comedians expect to enter shows for free. Even more confusing, fellow improvisors were shocked at the thought of complementary entry to shows and insisted that we charge everyone in attendance, except for the evening's performers. In improv culture, paying entrance fees indicates support; you always pay. We quickly realized that an all-female improv troupe running an open-mic night in the prairies was most certainly a comedy cultural hybrid that tested the patience of many local pros. Furthermore, some critics took to social media to air grievances against the troupe, posting tired conversations concerning the legitimacy of female comics; some claimed that women are not funny—"Women just aren't funny; it sucks, but it's true." In one surprising post, a well-known local comedian threatened physical violence should a female comedian fail to deliver well in her set. He claimed he would orchestrate physical beatings to unfunny women. Not surprisingly, his definition of "funny" was never clearly defined.

Much of the critique made against us is rooted in the more widely critical analysis of general feminist theory. Near the beginning of our troupe, a fellow improvisor who I had been working with for years articulated a desire to make an all-male team in response to LadyBits: "Well if you girls want to get away from us so bad, why do you care if we make a team of our own?" I feel that this statement was made in jest, but it does highlight underlying confusion about what feminist comedy really is. It made me question if LadyBits was reclaiming humour or simply replacing one rigid structure with another. Furthermore, identifying as a feminist comedy troupe can be fragile when individual members of the troupe each recognize and interact with feminist theory differently. Jenny is a robust feminist, well researched and ever well defined in her personal approach to feminist comedic performance. She often daydreams of facilitating an exercise wherein people gather together to smash plates printed with the word "patriarchy" across them. Courtney is self-critical and highly aware of her bias; she is always seeking deeper knowledge of what feminism really means to her and how she would like to implement it into her performance. We have spent many hours discussing the efficacy of satirizing gender roles, analyzing gendered roles, and debating if there are roles that harm women in comedy. I would like to say that I have always been feminist, but the embarrassing truth is that I have enculturated many behaviours and beliefs shaped directly as a product of living and working in a patriarchal society. Most of my knowledge about feminism came from trendy Instagram posts and misinterpreted *Hey Girl* memes featuring a smouldering Ryan Gosling in a tight white shirt, and I spent little time reflecting on my performances in critical and meaningful ways. Fields writes about early female comedians assuming submissive roles on stage: "They became props—attractive bimbos, nagging wives, neurotic mothers, or needy daughters—vehicles through which the 'take my wife home please' generation drove home their brand of humour" (xxiv). I can't tell you how many times I have played these characters. For years, I accepted less pay, reduced stage time, and taking a back seat in important group discussions for no other reason than I did not realize the subtle submissive role I assumed in those early days of performance. By not speaking up in those moments, I actively participated in the perpetuation of patriarchal behaviours. A regular LadyBits attendee happily articulated: "I love watching you three perform because you are all so different. Jenny is smart and cute, Courtney is sharp, and you [Marley] are so easygoing" (Person). Our individuality supports our collective performance. I think our varied understanding of what feminism is and how we should use it in our performance has been a strength rather than a weakness. Although any theory is stronger when practiced collectively, performance is highly subjective and personal, as is humour and comedy; thus, a reflection of any theory in performance will be varied.

LadyBits continues to focus on building community, capacity, and programming with a feminist lens. We remain dedicated to creating safe spaces for female and female-identified peoples and to share skills, to teach, to do outreach, and to learn. Mostly, we just want to make people laugh.

I am reminded of this when I do finally arrive at Amigos. The restaurant is bustling, its loud, and the smell of nachos hits me like new-wave feminism in a sleepy prairie town. The sign reads "Comedy Show Tonight!" I head to the backroom. Jenny is dancing in her chair as she eats her cheesy enchilada. Courtney hustles in, breathtaking as usual in her leather tights and crop top, waving the games list in her hand. There is already a lineup at the door. I stand in the middle of the room and let the electricity in the air crackle on my skin. It feels familiar; tonight is going to be lit.

Works Cited

Fields, Anna. *The Girl in the Show: Three Generations of Comedy, Culture, and Feminism.*: Arcade Publishing, 2017.

Gooijer, de Nicole. Personal interview. 26 Mar. 2018.

Person, Dillon. Personal interview. July 2018.

Rothenburger, Teri. Personal interview. 27 Dec. 2017.

Smith, Briony. "Women are Taking Over the World of Comedy." *Fashion Magazine*, 15 Sept. 2017, fashionmagazine.com/culture/women-taking-over-comedy/. Accessed 28 Dec. 2020.

CHAPTER 7

"Immoral, Slut, Arsehole": Feminist Memes Reclaim Stereotypes

Sai Amulya Komarraju

Introduction

In 2016, Sonam Mittal, an everyday Indian woman, faced a huge backlash for writing about two separate instances of sexual harassment and rape she experienced at her workplace and on vacation. She posted these accounts on *Youth Ki Awaaz*, a user-generated media portal. One blogger, who was particularly vicious in his trolling, blamed her for not realizing that "she also has a role to play in what happens to her," shifting the blame from the perpetrator to the survivor. He labelled her a "spoilt modern Indian woman [who] apes western women [and] wants all the freedoms but none of the responsibilities" (qtd in Purushatma). To reclaim the words "modern," often used pejoratively, and "spoilt," Mittal, along with Bruce Vain, started a Facebook page called "The Spoilt Modern Indian Woman"[1] (TSMIW henceforth) and called for fellow spoilt, modern Indian women to contribute to a feminist meme campaign to counter everyday sexism, misogyny, and patriarchal gender norms.

Although online spaces are increasingly being used to maintain the status quo (Madhabhushi et al. 46), Indian feminists are exploring multiple ways of doing feminism in the network (Rentschler and Thrift 332). "Networked feminism" (Fotopoulou 5) or "mediated feminisms" (Moorti 123) operate through the offline-online continuum of activism.

Examples from India include Jasmeen Patheja's Blank Noise project, which protested against street sexual harassment in 2003; the Pink Chaddi campaign, organized through the Facebook page "The Consortium of Pub-Going, Loose and Forward Women," which involved mailing pink panties to Shiv Ram Sene, a Hindu right-wing group that attacked pub goers in Karnataka in 2009; and the more recent nationwide "I Will Go Out" campaign in 2017, which protested against sexual harassment and became the rallying call around which women from many Indian cities marched in the streets to reclaim public space.

Apart from feminist blogs, Facebook pages and groups, as well as Twitter handles and hashtag activism, feminist memes, webcomics, and GIFs have emerged as specific forms of humour, irony, and satire in online spaces and are a fairly understudied phenomena, particularly in the Indian context. Defining feminist humour as "purposeful subversion of traditional expectations," Lizbeth Goodman notes that humour can resist rigid and traditional constructions of gender roles that tell "what women are" or "should be" (289). Sunithi Namjoshi's *Feminist Fables*[2] and Kamala Bhasin's *Laughing Matters*[3] are some of the examples of Indian feminist humour in English. More recently, the internet "has become a major actor in the production and distribution of humour" (Shifman, "Humour" 187), with webcomics, satirical parody news sites, and memes gaining popularity across social and cultural geographies.

By drawing on existing scholarship on feminist humour and internet memes, this chapter examines the content of TSMIW memes and historicizes the meme campaign to understand how the reification of essential femininity can be traced back to the nationalist project in India. It ultimately locates feminist humour as a part of a "radically new kind of feminist politics" (Kurian) that focuses on the vocabulary of rights and modes of protest in India. Finally, this chapter argues that TSMIW's "feminist détournement," or feminist reappropriation (Rentschler and Thrift 332) of existing norms through humour keeps politics hopeful and is a call for action against prevailing social mores by making everyday feminism the norm through the production and circulation of memes that smash everyday sexism.

Given the reasons for the emergence of the campaign, its content and context, it is important to note that the kind of feminism this chapter talks about—namely networked feminism or doing feminism in the network—is largely dominated by the English-speaking and urban Indian middle class.

Putting It into Context: The Emergence of Feminist Memes in India

In 2016, a series of humorous feminist memes in English by TSMIW went viral in India, drawing comparisons to the Everyday Sexism Project in the UK. The Everyday Sexism Project is a movement initiated by Laura Bates in 2012, which called on women to share their experiences on social media of "regular, run-of-the-mill, taken-for-granted, daily sexist moments that women encounter" but never talk about simply because it is "just a part of life—or, rather part of being a woman" (Bates). TSMIW memes address similar issues, among others.

Linda Shifman defines "internet meme" as a group of digital items, including image macros, Photoshopped photos, metaGIFs, YouTube videos, etc.; therefore, "meme" is always plural ("The Cultural Logic" 342). Memes share certain common characteristics in terms of content, form, or stance and are circulated and distributed online. Following Milika Trakilovic, this chapter refers to feminist memes as those memes concerned with "propagating feminism ... in the very midst of the workings of current popular and digital culture." TSMIW uses image macros, and in their "About" page on their website, the group identifies itself as an "inter-sectional feminist initiative that aims to challenge and break the innumerable gender related stereotypes which women, LGBTQ people, sexual minorities and men face in their everyday lives.[4] The "About" section on their Facebook page, however, reads, "Confining conditioning to hair follicles and eating patriarchy for dinner. Being a sexist bigot is gonna cost you but the laughs are free. P.S. Read page rules before posting."

TSMIW has an online presence beyond Facebook and a broader range of activities; their website offers feminist commentary on popular culture and sells streetwear and merchandise with some of their witty one-liners printed on them. This chapter, however, focuses on the feminist meme campaign on their Facebook page. The number of likes or reactions memes receive, as well as the ratings, reviews, captions, shares, and tags they garner, provide a dataset that is rich for analysis concerning the memes' popularity and impact.

The TSMIW Facebook page has 66,806 likes and 67,634 followers as of January 2021. They gained popularity through their first initiative, which called for their "fellow spoilt modern Indian women" to participate in fighting everyday sexism, misogyny, and gender norms through feminist memes. Instead of using a generic meme template, like those that are already available for replication or remixing, TSMIW crowdsourced photos that were voluntarily sent to them by everyday desi women. It is important to note that these women, in choosing to volunteer for this project, associated with it publicly. It is one of the first instances of a feminist social media campaign in India, where Indian women identified with the cause enough to choose to send their pictures. A comment on one of the memes reads, "Thank you, The Spoilt Modern Indian Woman, from an immoral, slut, arsehole. More power to you and all of us" (Acharjee). Later, in 2018, women from across India used a similar strategy to counter the sexist remarks of Manohar Parekhar, the then chief minister of Goa, who said girls drinking beer was a cause for concern. To express their ire over these comments, women posted selfies and ussies with the hashtag #GirlsWhoDrinkBeer, which trended on Twitter for several hours.

Calling women immoral, sluts, spoilt, or modern for transgressing boundaries can be traced back to the national project. Indian nationalists reconfigured gender roles by prioritizing essential femininity to modernize middle-class women and mark them as different from both white and working-class women in India, who were considered as sexual bodies by the middle classes. The establishment of "new patriarchy" by cultural revivalists of the nineteenth century during the national movement meant the reinforcement of the dichotomy of the public and private, or better known as ghar and bahir in India. The bahir came to be associated with public spaces, material culture and masculinity and ghar with the private and domestic spaces that also represent the spiritual and the feminine. Women were allowed to study and travel in order to fashion a "modern national culture" but were still required to perform "certain culturally visible spiritual qualities" in terms of their dress and social demeanour among other markers of purity as to not become Westernized (Chatterjee 622-31). These notions of purity are equated with asexual bodies, or bodies without desires. Such expectations of essential femininity continue to be of relevance today. For instance, Jyothi Singh, a gang-rape victim, was called "Nirbhaya" or "fearless" by the media because she fit the ideal victim prototype—a middle-class woman who died fighting her violators. Both the media coverage and the subsequent mobilization of the Indian middle classes to seek justice for "India's daughter" has since been critiqued by feminist scholars in

India (Komarraju and Raman 892). Particularly, feminist lawyer Flavia Agnes argues that Indians love "Nirbhaya" because she died fighting for her honour:

> In order to deserve our support, the victims must be without a blemish. They must die defending their honour. They must be larger than life, so we can honour and revere them. We hate those who survive to tell their tales of violations. Those who wish to live beyond the frame of victimhood.... The real women with a zest for life, with their sexualised bodies ... the memory of her ordinariness must be erased – the young woman with normal sexual desires and career ambitions, who seeks pleasures in visiting a mall or watching a movie with a male friend. She must now be sanitised, rendered into a blemishless sacrificial goat. Only then can she become worthy of our adoration. India's daughter.

As Nivedita Menon points out, patriarchal societies frame rape as a violation of one's honour; this is different from how feminists frame it—a violation of bodily autonomy (113). In 2015, just as Indians were recovering from the dreadful details of Singh's rape, Lesslie Udwin's documentary *India's Daughter* was released. In an article for the BBC, she quotes one of the lawyers defending the rapists as saying: "In our society, we never allow our girls to come out from the house after 6:30 or 7:30 or 8:30 in the evening with any unknown person....We have the best culture. In our culture, there is no place for a woman [in public spaces]" (M. L. Sharma qtd. in Udwin).

Although the comment was met with public outrage, such a mindset is symptomatic of the sensibility among the Indian middle class. Scholars have noted the continuing relevance of the sharp dichotomy between ghar and bahir, which frames public spaces as dangerous and, therefore, no place for decent women (Phadke, Khan, and Ranade). This mindset prompts a patriarchal stance of keeping women safe by both the family and the state rather than a rights-based response, which would encourage women's access to public spaces, bodily autonomy and sexual autonomy (Raman and Komarraju 14). It is against this backdrop that the TSMIW feminist memes must be studied in order to understand their potential as revolutionary feminist texts that offer resistance and space to circulate subversive messages.

Scope Of Feminist Memes

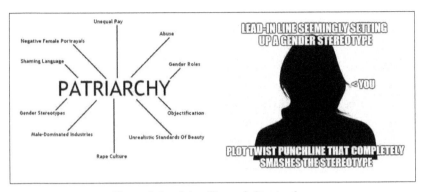

Figure 1. Lead-in; Figure 2. Patriarchy.

TSMIW's memes follow the template of using lead-ins—typically a stereotype, taboo, or norm—to which a feminist plot twist is added, which "completely smashes the stereotype" (Fig. 1). Several gender tropes and associated taboos are broken by TSMIW's memes. Figure 2 is a snapshot of the range of issues covered by the memes. One of the themes that emerges from examining these memes is that of a woman's right to public spaces. As discussed in the previous section, the dominant notion of women belonging to the ghar (domestic sphere) is turned on its head. While the lead-ins read variously as "I never go out alone" (Fig. 3), "I stay at home" (Fig. 4), or "I can't go out after 10" (Fig. 5), feminist punch-lines are added to reject these norms and show the possibilities of pleasure.

Figure 3. Alone; Figure 4. Home; Figure 5. Ten.

In their seminal work on loitering as a subversive practice in India, Shilpa Phadke, Sameera Khan, and Shilpa Ranade observe that women, even today, must adhere to certain rules, such as not being seen in public spaces without a legitimate reason and, to put it simply, never loitering for fun. When they do go out, they must perform the middle-class markers of dignity and purity to "manufacture respectability" and not attract unnecessary attention—be it through their purposeful strides (675-680) or by wearing a chunni, a cloth that goes around the neck and covers the chest (Raman and Komarraju).

Those women who do go out are labelled as spoilt, modern, and immoral, and they are held responsible for any harassment they may face. These norms are rejected by the memes through their template—pictures of smiling, carefree women who are comfortable in public spaces—and their feminist punchlines that normalize women's visibility in public spaces and show the possibilities of pleasure. This is especially important given the recent 2018 report by the Thomson Reuters Foundation, which marks India as the most unsafe country for women due to the high risk of sexual violence. As Phadke, Khan, and Ranade note, increasing crime rates result in a further clamping down of women's mobility and increased surveillance of their movements for their protection (201). Such a discourse of protection, either from the state or family, is often patriarchal and paternalistic and about controlling female sexuality.

Double Entendre and Female Sexuality

Another theme that emerges is that of using lead-ins that are sexual in nature, such as "My favorite position?" (Fig. 6) and "I am very flexible" (Fig. 7), with punchlines that have nothing to do with sex at all.

Figure 6. Position; Figure 7. Stretch.

In most South Asian societies, gender socialization operates in such a manner that male sexuality is promoted, whereas female sexuality is curtailed to preserve their virginity (Abraham 339). A woman's bodily honour is regarded as a symbol for the honour of not only her family but also her caste, community, and religion. Women are expected to maintain their virginity before marriage. According to this worldview, once she is married, a woman has a duty to have a monogamous sexual relationship with her husband and bear children (George 210).

Similarly, in her ethnographic research on women in the IT sector, Smitha Radhakrishanan illustrates how "new liberal Indian women," progressive in terms of education and employment, practice what she refers to as "respectable femininity"—such as marrying someone of their parents' choosing (keeping the lines of caste, class, and religion intact) and avoiding promiscuity (premarital sex or sex outside of marriage), which is "a product of 'Western' culture" (206). Even mainstream feminist discourse on sex in India is predominantly framed either around sexual reproduction and health or around sexual violence (such as rape, molestation, or dowries) (Turner 131-39). Such a framing, as important as it may be, does little to encourage women to explore their sexuality. What is missing from this either/or framework of abuse and health is the radical idea that sex can be fun and pleasurable for women.

Feminist humour is filling this lacuna, in which female sexuality and desire are discussed in a lighthearted, playful manner. This strategy creates awareness while packing a punch that smashes the patriarchal silence around the pleasurable element of sex. It also contributes to delinking sex from morality discourses and notions about what constitutes a good woman. Feminist humour tells women that it's okay to have sex, to enjoy sex, and to talk or, even better, joke about it. These memes break the idea that decent women must remain pure, spiritual, asexual, and in the domestic sphere. Although the lead-ins are sexual innuendos initiated by the women themselves, the punchlines used, though fairly mild, still illustrate that they are, in fact, in control of their sexuality and can pursue a variety of desires, such as becoming the prime minister or dancing in public.

Notions of Beauty

Although a richer body of literature on colourism exists, this chapter draws briefly on transnational feminist scholarship that is immediately relevant to the Indian context. Historically, light skin has been associated with divinity, upper caste mobility, beauty, and success, whereas dark skin is symbolic of evil, the lower castes, ugliness, and failure in India (Parameswaran and Cardoza 31). Apart from the caste system, India's colonial past, beauty pageants, Bollywood, advertisements, and patriarchy are some of the factors that have informed notions of beauty (Parameswaran; Runkle; Osuri). Meeta Jha examines the conflation of whiteness with being modern in India, the global rise of beauty industry, the liberalization and proliferation of skin-lightening products, and the cementing of the "idealization of whiteness" (9).

This preference for light skin, as Komal Kaur Dhillon notes, is also "a vehicle for fulfilling male fantasies of the ideal woman (in terms of beauty, morality, and prestige)" (8). Similarly, being slim is also a marker of desirability. Globalization and gendered beauty ideals have led to the demand for "fair-slim-beautiful" women, specifically in the context of matrimonial requirements (Ramasubramaniam and Jain 258).

The meme in Figure 8 pokes fun at the ideal of being thin in order to be desirable and adds a feminist plot-twist to "Find someone you like [and] Put their head in between your thighs," which suggests that the most desirable thigh gap is not associated with body size but rather being on the receiving end of enthusiastic oral sex.

Figure 8. Thigh Gap.

TSMIW memes with such lead-ins such "I want to be really fair" (Fig. 9) or "It's overwhelming when people tell me I'm that big" (Fig. 10) seek to destabilize the norm of linking beauty, described narrowly in terms of fairness and thinness, with success, achievement, and marriage by using feminist punchlines, such as being a fair judge or being an inspiration to others. These memes focus on desires and achievements, which do not emerge from the dominant narratives of beauty and femininity.

Figure 9. Fair: TSMIW; Figure 10. Big: TSMIW

Intersectionality

A broader overarching theme that both informs the creation of the memes and also emerges from the memes themselves is intersectionality (Crenshaw). TSMIW's original call for crowdsourcing pictures was addressed to women, and one commenter asked, "What about those who don't identify as women but are perceived as such by society?" In response to this, TSMIW amended their call and description to read: "So are you a Spoilt Modern Desi Woman? All desis who identify as women or are perceived as such by society—irrespective of body type, size, appearance, physical ability and gender assigned at birth—are welcome! Share this with everyone you know!"

Their intersectional stance is also reflected in the choice of using different templates for each meme. They recognize that women are not a homogenous category. A commenter on one of the memes questioned TSMIW as to why it did not follow the use of one template to make the meme more recognizable, to which the TSMIW replied:

Thanks for your suggestion but that's exactly what this isn't. The most important and recognisable aspect of this campaign is the crowdsourced photos. Using a template also says all women are same, they are not. Each has a different colour of skin, a different body size. Each has her own challenges, each is fighting a different battle. Yes, they [are] all fighting a common battle which comes with being a woman, but it will be unfair to use one template to represent them all. This is not Good Guy Greg, this is not Success Kid, this is Spoilt Modern Indian Women. Each is different, each is awesome.

They also make the case for intersectionality with two memes (Figs. 11 and 12).

Figure 11. Intersectionality; Figure 12. Headscarf.

One reads "I don't need feminism … without intersectionality." The meme serves two purposes. First, it pokes fun at people (including Bollywood actresses) who speak about gender equality but claim that they aren't feminists, and, second, it recognizes that multiple inter-sections of oppression form part of a feminist consciousness.

Another TSMIW meme (Fig. 12) features a Hijabi feminist at work, checking on her patient. It reads, "My headscarf is for safety… of my patients, because hair strands can be a surgery hazard." The person featured in the meme left a comment to clarify her position on the hijab: "So a lot of ppl ask me if you can wear a hijab and beat patriarchy… I say 'HELL yeah!!' Thank you The Spoilt Modern Indian Woman for making me a part of your campaign. Wearing what you wear, will not protect you no matter what, and ppl should stop forcing one to "dress decently" for safety." Furthermore, she writes in response to a comment not available anymore, "Yes. It [hijab] was apparently also for safety of women ... but I don't wear it for those [religious] reasons. It's just a headdress to me ... like someone else would wear a fedora."

Although it is true that most of these ideas about patriarchy and harmful notions about beauty and femininity are not unique to India, these issues must be contextualized because they are embedded within the cultural, social, and national fabric of India. Homi Bhabha notes that patriarchy must be "put in a relevant context" (81). Whereas patriarchy in the West intersects with warfare, gun culture, and racism, patriarchy in India operates along with caste and class lines, among other elements. To put it simply, patriarchy is neither uniform nor monolithic; its practices and ideas vary across contexts and cultures.

Feminist Humour: Politics of Possibility

Although the lead-ins used in TSMIW memes are common gender norms and stereotypes, and the group runs the risk of seeming as though they are endorsing them, feminist punchlines hijack the dominant narratives and insert plot-twists that turn the table—a strategy described as "feminist detournement" by Rentschler and Thrift (332). Although recent literature suggests that humour can be an attempt to turn laughter into anger and engagement (Moorti 122), these memes instead emerge from anger as the starting point, which is then turned into laughter to call out the ridiculousness of cultural expectations based on gender and show the possibilities of agency—of not just talking back to stereotypes but also rejecting them.

Whereas mainstream feminist archiving, such as the Everyday Sexism Project, focus on daily sexism (Chamberlain 119), TSMIW memes reject the traumatic and protectionist frameworks, such as the state's response to violence against women (Raman and Komarraju 1), and keep feminist politics and activism playful and "hopeful rather than resigned and bitter" (Kaufman 8). The kind of humour employed by TSMIW shares *some* characteristics with "charged humour" (Krefting). Although the context of charged humour is stand-up comedy and cultural citizenship, I borrow this this term insofar as it means "doing" something proactively to address inequality (Krefting 2). Rebecca Krefting's "charged humour" refers to "comedic material ... literal in meaning and explicit in politics," which calls for mobilization (Kein 674, 675). TSMIW memes are also quite literal and political, and the creators of TSMIW, along with the contributors of the pictures, accuse the public with perpetuating social and cultural injustices. The serious potential of feminist memes, then, is in their hopefulness—in showing women the possibilities that exist along with anger, trauma, or burden of remembering (Fig. 13).

Figure 13. Culture.

By Way of Conclusion

Since "content-related jokes ... require shared views" (Katthoff 17), these pages and websites are followed by people who have internet access and who are interested in receiving such information. This means that although spaces such as TSMIW bring together like-minded feminists, there is always the risk of creating echo chambers, where these conversations are limited to those who are already in on the joke and who already subscribe to these views. Moreover, because of the short shelf life of memes on the internet (Baran 172), feminists must keep creating new content to keep these conversations relevant and accessible to the wider public.

TSMIW is only one instance of a self-identified feminist platform that draws on irony and humour in India. There are many other sites of humour, such as Feminism in India's meme campaign to reclaim the #NotAllMen used by Men's Rights Activists (MRAs); Aditi Mittal's[5], stand-up comedy content on YouTube, which breaks taboos around menstruation; and Agents of Ishq's multimedia project, which often uses humour to make conversations around female sexuality, desire, and sex less awkward. These examples energize "current feminisms" by providing space for feminist engagement with the issues outlined above (Rentschler and Thrift 335).

The Justice Verma committee, constituted to suggest changes to the legal framework after the aforementioned gang rape of Jyothi Singh in 2012, emphatically states that the "Correction of the societal mindset of its gender bias depends more on social norms, and not merely on legal sanction" (ii-iii). Whereas "mainstream feminism" addresses serious issues (Kurian)—such as dowries, domestic violence, and explicit forms of abuse—through legal recourse, TSMIW's memes address not only everyday sexism, misogyny, body shaming, victim shaming, victim blaming, and rape culture, but also the right to loiter, periods, desire, and sex. Ultimately, they work towards keeping feminist politics hopeful by changing social mores in a playful manner, one meme at a time.

Endnotes

1. www.facebook.com/spoiltmodernwoman/
2. Suniti Namjoshi is an Indian poet and is famous for her witty work, *Feminist Fables*, a reworking of fairy tales from the East and the West.
3. Kamala Bhasin is an Indian feminist activist who authored *Laughing Matters*, a feminist jokebook, with illustrations by Bindia Thapar.
4. www.spoiltmodernwoman.com (Between the writing of this chapter and its publication, their website has become defunct).
5. Aditi Mittal is an Indian stand-up comic.

Works Cited

Abraham, Leena. "Bhai-behen True Love, Time :ass: Friendships and Sexual Partnerships among Youth in an Indian Metropolis." *Culture, Health & Sexuality*, vol. 4, no. 3, 2002, pp. 337-53.

Acharjee, Dimpy. "Immoral, Slut, Arsehole." *Facebook*, 25 Apr. 2016, www.facebook.com/spoiltmodernwoman/photos/a.471649666360366/472614732930526. Accessed 5 September 2020.

Agnes, Flavia. "Why India Loves Nirbhaya, Hates Suzette." *Early Times Asian Age*, 20 Mar. 2015, www.earlytimes.in/newsdet.aspx?q=145524. Accessed 14 Oct. 2019.

Baran, Anneli. "Visual humour on the Internet." *Estonia and Poland: Creativity and Tradition in Cultural Communication*, edited by. L.

Laineste, D. Brzozowska, and W. Chłopicki, ELM Scholarly Press, 2012, pp. 171-86.

Bates, Laura. *Everyday Sexism.* Schuster & Schuster, 2014.

Bhabha, Homi K. "Liberalism's Sacred Cow." *Is Multiculturalism Bad for Women,* edited by Joshua Cohen et al., Princeton University Press, 1999, pp. 79-84.

Bhasin, Kamla, and Bindia Thapar. *Laughing <atters.* Jagori, 2004.

Chamberlain, Prudence. *The Feminist Fourth Wave: Affective Temporality.* Springer, 2017.

Chatterjee, Partha. "Whose Imagined community?" *Mapping the Nation,* edited by G. Balakrishnan, Verso, 1996, pp. 214-25.

Crenshaw, Kimberlé. "Mapping the Margins: Intersectionality, Identity Politics, and Violence against Women of Color." *Stanford Law Review,* vol. 43, no. 6, 1990, pp. 1241-99.

Dhillon, Komal Kaur. *Brown Skin, White Dreams: Pigmentocracy in India.* Dissertation. Virginia Tech, 2015, https://vtechworks.lib.vt.edu/handle/10919/73702. Accessed 30 Dec. 2020.

Fotopoulou, Aristea. "Digital and Networked by Default? Women's Organisations and the Social Imaginary of Networked Feminism." *New Media & Society,* vol. 18, no. 6, 2016, pp. 989-1005.

George, Annie. "Embodying Identity through Heterosexual Sexuality-Newly Married Adolescent Women in India." *Culture, Health & Sexuality,* vol. 4, no. 2, 2002, pp. 207-22.

Goodman, Lizbeth. "Gender and Humour." *Imagining Women: Cultural Representations and Gender,* edited by Frances Bonner et al., Polity Press, 1992, pp. 286-300.

Jha, Meeta R. *The Global Beauty Industry: Colorism, Racism, and the National Body.* Routledge, 2016.

Kaufman, Gloria J., Ed. *In Stitches: A Patchwork of Feminist Humour and Satire.* Indiana University Press, 1991.

Kein, Kathryn. "Recovering Our Sense of Humour: New Directions in Feminist Humour Studies." *Feminist Studies,* vol. 41, no. 3, 2015, pp. 671-81.

Komarraju, Sai Amulya, and Usha Raman. "Indian Millennials Define Feminism." *Feminist Media Studies,* vol. 17, no. 5, 2017, pp. 892-96.

Krefting, Rebecca. *All Joking Aside: American Humour and Its Discontents.* JHU Press, 2014.

Kurian, Alka. "#MeToo Is Riding a New Wave of Feminism in India." *The Conversation*, 1 Feb. 2018, theconversation.com/metoo-is-riding-a-new-wave-of-feminism-in-india-89842. Accessed 14 Oct. 2019.

Menon, Nivedita. *Seeing Like a Feminist.* Penguin UK, 2012.

Moorti, Sujata. "Indignant Feminism: Parsing the Ironic Grammar of *YouTube* Activism." *Emergent Feminisms*, edited by Jessalynn Keller and Maureen E. Ryan, Routledge, 2018, pp. 120-37.

Namjoshi, Sunita. *Feminist Fables.* Sheba Feminist Publishers, 1981.

Osuri, Goldie. "Ash Coloured Whiteness: The Transfiguration of Aishwarya Rai." *South Asian Popular Culture*, vol. 6, no. 2, 2008, pp. 109-23.

Parameswaran, Radhika. "Global Beauty Queens in Post-Liberalization India." *Peace Review: A Journal of Social Justice*, vol. 17, no. 4, 2005, pp. 419-26.

Parameswaran, Radhika E., and Kavitha Cardoza. "Immortal Comics, Epidermal Politics: Representations of Gender and Colorism in India." *Journal of Children and Media*, vol. 3, no. 1 2009, pp. 19-34.

Phadke, Shilpa, Sameera Khan, and Shilpa Ranade. *Why Loiter?: Women and Risk on Mumbai Streets.* Penguin Books India, 2011.

Purushatma. "Sonam Mittal is the spoilt modern Indian woman." *Purushatma: The Politically-Incorrect Blog for the Indian Man*, 12 June 2015, purushatma.wordpress.com/2015/06/12/sonam-mittal-is-the-spolit-modern-indian-woman/. Accessed 6 July 2018.

Radhakrishnan, Smitha. "Professional Women, Good Families: Respectable Femininity and the Cultural Politics of a 'New' India." *Qualitative Sociology*, vol. 32, no. 2, 2009, pp. 195-212.

Raman, Usha, and Sai Amulya Komarraju. "Policing Responses to Crime against Women: Unpacking the Logic of Cyberabad's 'SHE Teams.'" *Feminist Media Studies*, vol. 18, no. 4, 2018, pp. 718-33.

Ramasubramanian, Srividya, and Parul Jain. "Gender Stereotypes and Normative Heterosexuality in Matrimonial Ads from Globalizing India." *Asian Journal of Communication*, vol. 19, no. 3, 2009, pp. 253-69.

Rentschler, Carrie A., and Samantha C. Thrift. "Doing Feminism in the Network: Networked Laughter and the 'Binders Full of Women' Meme." *Feminist Theory*, vol. 16, no. 3, 2015, pp. 329-59.

Runkle, Susan. "Making 'Miss India.' Constructing Gender, Power and the Nation." *South Asian Popular Culture*, vol. 2, no. 2, 2004, pp. 145-59.

Shifman, Limor. "Humour in the Age of Digital Reproduction: Continuity and Change in Internet-Based Comic Texts." *International Journal of Communication*, vol. 1, no. 1, 2007, pp. 187-209.

Shifman, Limor. "The Cultural Logic of Photo-Based Meme Genres." *Journal of Visual Culture*, vol. 13, no. 3, 2014, pp. 340-58.

Thomson Reuters Foundation. "The World's 10 Most Dangerous Countries for Women." *Opinion Poll*, 2018, poll2018.trust.org/. Accessed 15 Oct. 2019.

Trakilovic, Milika. "Hey Girl: Who Needs Feminism? Feminism as a Meme." *Journal of Art and Digital Culture*, vol. 28, 2013, dpi.studioxx.org/en/no/28-gendered-cultures-internet/hey-girl-who-needs-feminism-feminism-meme. Accessed 31 July 2018.

Turner, Elen. "Indian Feminist Publishing and the Sexual Subaltern." *Rupkatha Journal*, vol. 1, no. 1, 2014, pp. 131-41.

Udwin, Leslee. "Delhi Rapist Says Victim Shouldn't Have Fought Back." *BBC*, 5 Mar. 2015, www.bbc.com/news/magazine-31698154. Accessed 31 July 2018.

Chapter Eight

Queens of the Castle: Intergenerational Conversations about Elaine Benes's (Imperfect) Feminism

Stephanie Patrick and Hayley R. Crooks

Introduction

Our moms love Elaine Benes from *Seinfeld*. As the lone woman on one of the most popular sitcoms of all time, Elaine, played by comedian Julia Louis-Dreyfus, has often been invoked as signifier of the new gender equality achieved by urban, middle-class, white women of the 1990s (Hirsch and Hirsch). However, Elaine's parity is almost as often read as being "masculine" (Di Mattia 68), with "*excessive* appetites for food and sex" (our emphasis, Morreale 283). Elaine's gendered position within the show is a precarious one, as she alternately occupies various roles in relation to feminism: the feminist, the sex symbol, the average woman, and the killjoy. Whether or not *Seinfeld* is a misogynist show (as argued by Hirsch and Hirsch 120), it is certainly a patriarchal one, centred as it is on the anxieties, desires, and shortcomings of modern urban (Jewish) men in the United States (Cooper; Di Mattia). Elaine's efforts to navigate through that patriarchal world makes her a notable and underexamined site of feminist politics in relation to comedy.

Despite co-creator Larry David's "no hugging, no learning" credo (Morreale 278), Elaine served for us, growing up, as a character with both sentimental and educational potential. As young women born in the 1980s (Hayley in Ontario; Stephanie in Alberta), Elaine Benes served as a uniquely fallible aspirational character, shaping our own understandings of contemporary gender relations in ways that were markedly different from those of our mothers'. Although we both found our way to feminist scholarship through different paths, as PhD colleagues, we discovered a shared connection over the role that humour plays in our relationships with feminism(s), with Elaine figuring prominently in our early popular culture consumption as an icon of feminism and femininity.

Using this character as a conduit, we each conducted one semi-structured interview with our mothers about *Seinfeld* in order to understand how they situate Elaine within ideas of feminist humour. Furthermore, we were interested in learning about generational differences that we believed might surface through comparing our mothers' readings of Elaine with our own. Each interview lasted approximately one and a half hours, and both flowed freely between episodes and—in Erica and Stephanie's case—to different cultural touchstones. We additionally weave in some autoethnographic reflections on these conversations with our mothers, which allows for a deeper analysis of intergenerational understandings of and relationships to feminism while providing one of the few reception-based studies of this classic sitcom.

Our mothers' identities inform their reading of *Seinfeld* and their relationship to feminism more broadly. Hayley's mother, Monica, grew up in the Northern Canadian town of Rouyn-Noranda, Québec, during the 1950s and 1960s. She graduated as a registered nurse in 1971 and worked in Ontario hospitals (surgical, obstetrics, and psychiatry) until the early 1990s, when she decided to become the primary caregiver to her daughter with severe childhood asthma. She then continued to work outside the home part time in youth and community programming as well as alternative health services. Stephanie's mother Erica grew up in the small city of Red Deer, Alberta, in the 1960s and 1970s. She moved to the city of Calgary as a young adult and had married and given birth to her daughter Stephanie by the early 1980s. She has worked fulltime outside of the home for her entire adult life, mostly in office settings across several different industries.

It is worth also briefly outlining our various audience positions in relation to the *Seinfeld* text more broadly. Whereas Hayley is undoubtedly the biggest fan of us all (she owns the entire series on DVD, has watched the behind-the-scenes extras, and read *Seinfeldia* upon its release), Stephanie's mother, Erica, is the other (but lesser) fan of the bunch (as she has watched most episodes numerous times both upon initial airing and in syndication). We, therefore, have inverse relationships to *Seinfeld* fandom with our mothers: Stephanie's mother is a bigger fan and expert on *Seinfeld* than she is, whereas Hayley's mother is less of a fan and will rely upon Hayley's recall of the show more in her interview. As Stephanie and Hayley grew to know each other, Elaine Benes became an obvious focal point for understanding how humour shapes ours and our mothers' (intergenerational) understandings of feminism as well as the possibilities Elaine suggests for future representations of women characters in popular culture.

Elaine as a Cultural Figure

Although there has been academic work on *Seinfeld* in relation to Jewishness (Brook; Cooper) and gender (Cooper; Di Mattia), there has been less focus on female identity and feminist politics in the show. The character of Elaine has alternately appeared in other research contexts: messages about female sexual pleasure ("Sexual Stereotypes"); hostile customers in relation to hospitality industries, wherein Elaine represents the hostile customer (Pizam); discussions of pedagogy that use the J. Peterman catalogue, where Elaine worked for several seasons, to teach students about visual literacy (Seglam and Witte); and the effects of thin representations of women on disordered eating, wherein Elaine stood for the average woman (Harrison).

Perhaps because of her distance from both feminist politics and female-oriented (or female-centred) popular culture texts, Elaine is not often mentioned in broader discussions of feminist comedy. Moreover, feminist analyses of sitcoms have traditionally focused on relationships between women and men revolving around the "heterosexual script" (Kim et al.) or on female-driven shows (Dow; Lee). Although recent sitcoms may have more obvious connections to feminist politics, the

1980s was not only a time of economic conservatism but also an era of cultural and political backlash against the second-wave feminist movements of the 1960s and 1970s. Female comics and female-driven comedy shows aired in the United States and Canada (e.g., *Roseanne*, *Murphy Brown*, and *Designing Women*), but they existed in a context that was not particularly welcoming to feminists or to progressive content. However, the focus in such sitcoms on women's lives across the home-workplace divide (a divide often used in sitcom genealogy) spoke precisely to the so-called gains won by the earlier generation of feminists and, as noted by Lauren Rabinovitz, often presented a range of feminist politics and subjectivities, both celebrating and problematizing women's place in the workforce and family (Grabowski).

Whereas female-driven shows—which are often conflated with both female-oriented shows and feminist shows (see Swink)—depicted home and work life, female characters in male-driven sitcoms often sat on the sidelines, serving in the classic role of the wife or love interest to the main character. This was not the case for *Seinfeld*'s Elaine Benes, who is introduced as a former love interest for Jerry but plays an equal role as the other three male friends centred in the sitcom. Although Elaine is never explicitly identified as a feminist (the closest she gets is yelling "I hate men, but I'm not a lesbian!" on the subway ["The Subway"]), she functions for some female viewers, according to our research, as the feminist symbol of equality in a male-dominated sitcom.[1] Elaine Benes offers a realistic—if somewhat farcical—view of the working lives of single, middle-class, urban, white women in the late 1980s and early 1990s.

Initially *Seinfeld*'s lone female character was a waitress played by Lee Garlington, but after apparently angering Larry David, she was fired with the network requesting a stronger female presence on the show (Armstrong 40-41). Although they had suggested bringing in Elaine as Jerry's girlfriend, David's writing her in as an ex-girlfriend provided much more comedic and narrative potential. Despite, or perhaps precisely because she was, being written by men (a notable exception here is the work of Carol Leifer on twenty-three episodes), Elaine stood out on the sitcom landscape for her equal status to the men surrounding her. Although the threat of feminism underlies her strong character (and this threat is most often represented through the character of George who is admittedly afraid of her), it is contained by the writing of the show and the performance of Julia Louis-Dreyfus, which often comedically both celebrates and undermines the dangers of a smart, successful, and hegemonically attractive woman, who has (sometimes) achieved gender equality. In this way, *Seinfeld* portrays gender equality (in a typically postfeminist sense) while offering an aspirational model for it—one in which female characters are judged not for their domestic abilities or for their attractiveness to men but for their ability to run a clothing company, for their taste in films, or even for the spongeworthiness of their lovers. This, in turn, potentially explains the appeal of a male-driven show and the character of Elaine to feminist-identifying pop culture lovers like us and our mothers, all of whom display different understandings of and relations to feminism and comedy while agreeing on our love of all things Elaine.

Elaine, Monica, and Erica

Previous work on *Seinfeld* reveals how important it is to situate the text in relation to the audience watching it, especially in terms of character. This position is clear in the various readings of Elaine as not Jewish (Brook 60; Hirsch and Hirsch 118); as signifying Jewishness despite textual references to the contrary (Cooper 98); or as being part of a cast of "white, heterosexual, middle-class New Yorkers" (Di Mattia 62). Neither of us nor our mothers have ever perceived Elaine as being Jewish. When asked about Elaine's background, for example, Stephanie's mother, Erica, drew upon her memory of one of the only *Seinfeld* episodes featuring Elaine's family ("The Jacket"):

> I never really thought about [her background], but there was that episode where Jerry and George met her Dad, and she was late, and he was so scary. That made me think that Elaine probably grew up in a privileged background. A very strong father figure. I don't know anything about her mom. They never said anything about her mother. But that, that she was used to having that strong male presence in her life which made her very comfortable with George and Jerry or, and Kramer or whatever.

That Erica only decoded Elaine's identity in terms of class and gender speaks to her own experiences as a white, middle-class, fourth generation settler woman living in Canada. For Hayley—who is a white, middle-class, Canadian woman—the episode about Elaine's "shiksappeal" (a "shiksa" is a non-Jewish woman) stands out to her as distinguishing Elaine's background from the Jewish characters on the show (although the casting of Louis-Dreyfus in that role, who is herself Jewish, as well as other signifying elements of the show, explain the ambiguity). When Hayley asked Monica about Elaine's background, it was clear she did not view Elaine as coming from a specific cultural lens: "Aside from the curly hair ... and she certainly wears unusual clothes for a grown woman, I've never seen her as part of any ethnic groups at all because her hair is so curly you do wonder if there's some ethnic background there." It is worth noting that both Erica and Monica focused their analyses of the relationships they see between Elaine, feminism, and comedy within strictly gendered frameworks, which focus mostly on the representations of Elaine's relationships and sexuality.

Although Erica would not consider herself as privileged as Elaine, Stephanie assumed she would have related to the character as a working woman. Again, there are various readings of Elaine's relations to the world of work. Some critics view her as being "the only main character who held a steady job" (Morreale 281), although she did change jobs regularly, whereas other critics assert that Elaine "has no ambition and uses her wiles to avoid serious work" (Hirsch and Hirsch 118). However, while Erica did extensively discuss work in various contexts, she did not draw on Elaine as an example of a working woman on television as much as she did Mary Tyler Moore from *The Mary Tyler Moore Show*, perhaps because Moore's character spoke directly to specific feminist workplace issues. When asked about depictions of working women, Erica recalled:

> We watched an episode [of *The Mary Tyler Moore Show*] on TV not that long ago, where [Mary] went in to talk to her boss about a pay discrepancy between her and some other guy doing the same job. And he was explaining to her why that was, and then she was trying to explain to him why that was not valid. And this was from the 1970s! And I don't remember that episode ever being controversial; it must have been at the time, but when I saw it like two months ago, it was like, "woah! This was on TV?!" It wouldn't even go on TV today.

This comment came at a point in the discussion of 1980s sitcoms depicting working women (e.g., *Murphy Brown*, *Designing Women*, and

Kate & Allie), demonstrating—in Erica's eyes at least—the ways in which progress in representation is not necessarily linear. For Erica, feminist representations of working women in the 1970s were more progressive than depictions she is seeing on contemporary television. It is interesting then, as will be shown later, that all of her favourite Elaine moments and episodes were dealing with relationships and sexuality more than they were her workplace. On the contrary, some of Stephanie's favourite Elaine moments were working ones, particularly from her time working at the J. Peterman catalogue.

Defining Feminism

In her interview, Erica displays a complex relationship with feminism, perhaps reflecting some of the broader ambivalences surrounding the term. Although Erica described herself as having "always been a feminist," she also remembered the *Seinfeld* era (late 1980s to early 1990s) as being, for her, a time when she was too busy to think about feminism: "Life was kind of in the way of theoretical things in those days. It was just, there was just too much to do every day to think about that kind of thing, so it wasn't really on my radar at the time. I was just a normal working mom. Too busy to think about things like feminism." For Erica, the theoretical aspects of feminism were too far removed from her day-to-day life for her to consider them relevant, which likely influenced Stephanie's own distance from feminism growing up. Despite being surrounded by such feminist tomes as *Backlash* (Faludi), Stephanie refused to identify as a feminist until she was in graduate school. Interestingly, Erica felt responsible for this disidentification: "When I think about that I think 'oh my god, how could I have let that happen?!' But it wasn't, like I say, it wasn't something that I'd think about on a day-to-day basis. I was too frickin' busy!"

Monica's response when asked about her perceptions of second-wave feminism spoke to how she situated herself concerning that moment in the women's movement.

> I don't think [growing up in the 1960s] I was aware that some of the ways I was treated were having to do with the fact I was a girl, not a boy. I don't think I was very conscious of that, so it wasn't until the 70s that I became aware of the women's movement at all…. Um, [laughter] I think it was very confusing because I think

a lot of people felt it was about burning their brassieres or something. There was a lot of talk in my time about women should burn their brassieres and all these things, and I think we didn't really realize this was supposed to be about equal pay for equal work and things like that rather than, you know, the sensationalism of actually going without your brassiere. I mean I realize as I'm talking to you I did have a period of time where I just didn't wear a brassiere and that was considered just astoundingly brazen, so instead of burning mine, I just didn't wear one for a while. But that was pretty short lived. That was my little rebellion. I think it lasted about a month.

After this reflection on her brief moment in the sun as a "braless wonder" ("The Caddy"), Hayley asked her mother—a much more casual viewer than Hayley—what specifically she likes about Elaine. She clearly articulated her adoration of what she viewed as Elaine's comic feminist persona. Monica loved Elaine's authentic style but struggled with whether or not the humorous traits she loved the most about Elaine marked the character as a feminist for her. For Monica, most of the feminist potential in Elaine came from what she saw as a flagrant disregard for the most stringent rules women of her generation were bound to follow. Her descriptions of specific Elaine moments that stand out for her hinged around two central themes: Elaine's ability to choose her own life and the character's overt sexuality. These themes highlight the way Monica situates Elaine and her hilarity:

> I guess because she just seems like somebody who doesn't live by other people's judgments, yet she knows when people are judging her. She makes these little gestures and faces when she knows that she's going to be judged, or she's being judged but she goes ahead anyway. She doesn't let it stop her from saying what she thinks from what is her truth regardless, and yet she indicates by her facial expressions a lot of the time that she knows that what she's saying is going to be considered, you know, out of bounds or out of the norm for whatever she's talking about.

In the passage above, it is clear that Monica links what she identifies as Elaine's fulfilment of her own life choices to the feminist impulse Elaine displays in seeing the disapproval of others yet sticking with her choice anyways. The way Monica reads Elaine's disregarding of traditional feminine norms through gesture in this passage underscores the feminist humour that the character brings to *Seinfeld*. For Monica, it is Elaine's breaching of these daily implied gendered social norms that give her humour a distinctly feminist quality. It is notable that Elaine's (bourgeois) feminism is (from Monica's perspective) unique in its everyday woman authenticity, yet it still glamorizes middle-class women's work as the ultimate achievement, thus realizing the hopes of second-wave feminism. Elaine's portrayal can be understood in contrast to representations of working-class women depicted in *Roseanne*, who came to signify, for many women, a fantasy of working-class women's self-worth "in a world where they have little control" (Bettie).

Erica's view on Elaine's feminism differed slightly, signalled not by Elaine's authenticity or freedom (of choice) but by her status in relation to the men in the program: "Yes, I think she is [a feminist]. She considers herself the equal of all the men she runs into on the show." She saw Elaine as being "different" from George, Jerry, and Kramer but, at the same time, being their friend: "They trust her, and she trusts them." As an example of this trust, Erica specifically noted the scene in which Jerry and George ask Elaine if women know about male "shrinkage" ("The Hamptons"). To her, this illustrated the ways in which the men perceived Elaine as their equal. This reading of Elaine's gender equality is particularly interesting in light of Erica's earlier comments about feminism as something that was too theoretical to be relevant to her day-to-day life. Perhaps what marks Elaine's feminism as relatable to Erica is precisely that she was living equality rather than theorizing it (or articulating it in a more academic or political way). One of the most significant things about Elaine as a cultural character, then, is that she so easily embodies a relatable popular feminism.

Spongeworthy

For Monica, Hayley's mother, Elaine is a feminist because she represents someone that makes her own choices—especially when they go against the grain of proper or hegemonic femininity—and is sexually liberated. For Monica, this means Elaine plans for "her own pleasure" and is unashamed in seeking out spongeworthy situations. Interestingly, an episode that stood out for both of our mothers was

"The Sponge." In fact, it is this episode that Monica cited when asked to give a specific example of Elaine's feminism:

> Yes, I think the one especially where she wants the sponge for birth control, and she goes out of her way to find them and then she stocks up with all these sponges, and she's so open about it, I think. I don't know if that means she's a feminist, but it gives you the feeling that she is because she's open about her sexuality and the fact that she enjoys it and that she's thinking ahead. Women of my generation were raised to think "Oh you would never think that far ahead, you would never." That would be admitting that you were planning to have sex and that you had to be prepared with all that birth control rather than "Oh you just got carried away in the moment" because that's the way we were raised.... You could sort of understand if someone got carried away but to have planned that far ahead and to be that open about your enjoyment of sex was, for my generation—that wasn't really what we were supposed to do.

The episode addresses the impossible contradictions in rules policing proper femininity head on when Jerry is horrified to find that the closet of his goody-two-shoes girlfriend, Lena, is full of boxes of the Today sponge. Jerry had viewed her as a good girl, who volunteers for charity causes—someone with whom he cannot even envision having sex ("You can't have sex with someone you admire. Where's the depravity?"). Jerry's reaction after finding the sponges represents what Monica described about the sexual codes of conduct for women of her generation. Now Jerry cannot imagine continuing to date Lena ("Oh my God! Look at what's going on here! She's depraved!"). Monica's evocation of this episode focused on the dual themes of choice and sexual liberation, which could make women viewers that grew up in her generation jealous. Monica pointed to this explanation for why Elaine may be regarded by many viewers as a flawed or unacceptable:

> I feel these days she would be considered more acceptable, but ...I feel yeah I don't know how other women of my generation would feel about her, but they might feel jealous that she was that liberated. I think for a woman of my generation, we were brought up to not really be approving of someone like Elaine. So, you

have to get used to the fact that Elaine is her own woman and maybe Elaine is a character that brings home to people in my generation that we're not really feminists when we see a character like Elaine [who] really does what she wants to do.... [And] you really start to like Elaine because she's authentic, she's herself, and she doesn't seem to be living by anybody else's playbook.

Our mothers' diverging views on this episode, in particular, reveal the generational and perhaps social differences between them. For Monica, this episode stood out for Elaine's somewhat radical relationship to sex (presuming that she would seek out sex enough to prepare herself for it), whereas Erica, in particular, enjoyed the ways in which this episode realistically portrayed the uneven distribution of labour that goes into pregnancy prevention, not just in Elaine's private life but for George as well: "I also liked, on that episode too, that Susan confronted George 'cause he didn't know what kind of birth control she used." For Erica, her own experiences of uneven labour distribution across gender was a recurring theme, so not only does it make sense that she would be drawn to this particular episode (wherein Elaine gets to decide which men are worthy of not only her attraction but also of her very limited supply of contraception), but also that the most important aspect of Elaine's equality was her being one of the guys and, thus, escaping some of the trappings of domesticity. Perhaps this also explains the reasons that Erica was more drawn to depictions of Elaine's personal life rather than her working life, where she did have considerable responsibilities and stresses.

Appearance

One thing regarding Elaine's professional life that did stand out to Erica was her wardrobe. Erica thought that Elaine's clothes reflected an authenticity not seen in many contemporary representations of working women: "I loved that she always was in flat shoes, or just the tiniest little heel. To me, Elaine's clothing was always authentic, which made her, to me, more likeable because her clothing did look like clothes you would see on the street or you would wear. Not like the things that you see now." Of course, as a woman working in the 1980s,

Erica had a specific and situated idea of what authentic working women wore. The fact that Elaine's wardrobe reflected what "you would see on the street" suggests a less aspirational character than, for a comparative example that arose in our conversation, *House of Cards'* Claire Underwood. This realism of Elaine's 1980s style wardrobe in itself could demarcate Elaine as a feminist character—that she was not created to cater to a male gaze or to be an aspirational (fashion) figure who inspires women to self-improve through consumption (not that there's anything wrong with that!).[2] Elaine was just, in Erica's view, "somebody you could picture having for a friend" and was, therefore, authentic.

Monica repeatedly referred to Elaine as an "authentic feminist person" who lives in the moment. However, as someone who worked professionally in a medical setting and then split time between primary childcare and community-based work outside of the home, she described, with genuinely amused bafflement, that Elaine's clothing choices were something she could not relate to because she had not seen them before. Between fits of giggles, Monica pointed to Elaine's wardrobe—a detail she thought was representative of Elaine's ability to chart a unique path but one that also may not be realistic, saying "She certainly wears unusual clothes for a grown woman!"

Again, this contrasted with Erica who focused on Elaine's wardrobe as one of the many believable details that makes Elaine come to life as an example of 1980s and 1990s feminist womanhood. Perhaps this difference can be understood through the age gap between when Erica and Monica entered the workforce as well as the medical setting where Monica worked, where everyone wore uniforms. Whereas Elaine wears clothes that Erica may have seen worn by women in her office setting, many popular culture representations of women's fashion—such as Monica's favourite nighttime drama in the 1980s, *Knots Landing* (1979–1993)—tended to feature lighter pastel colours for women and the iconic large shoulder pad. Of course, these popular representations of women's clothing aligned with common visual representations of the dichotomy between feminism and femininity, as evidenced by programs such as *Murphy Brown* (Dow 148).[3]

The comments on Elaine's New York (rather than Los Angeles-based) style are not meant to suggest that Elaine does not have any sexual appeal or vanities. Despite the unpretentiousness of her wardrobe, Erica mentioned the fact that Elaine knew she had great hair: "[I liked] the fact that she didn't talk about but was always very proud of her hair. Remember that BO [body odour] smell, and it got in the car, and it got in her hair, and she had to get it washed, and she was all self-conscious about it or whatever" ("The Smelly Car"). Stephanie's mother Erica also zeroed in on the episode in which Elaine felt the need to prove to Jerry and George that, if she really wanted to, she could "put the butts in the seats"[4] with her cleavage ("The Shoes"). Elaine could be one of the guys but could also tap into and leverage her ability to perform (hegemonic) femininity in humorous ways (for she never did that without some comedic purpose). That she did not constantly feel the need to do this—and that this was not even remotely her purpose on the show—only made her character more appealing to all of us.

Conclusion ("Yada Yada Yada")

Although this chapter only begins to unravel the complex ways in which Elaine performed and embodied feminism, it is clear that she serves for some as a unique, if somewhat contradictory, figure of female empowerment. For white middle-class women like our mothers growing up (and living through young adulthood) in the era of second-wave feminism, Elaine's ability to choose, her disruption of norms, and her gender parity all signalled a shift in gender relations that reflected real-life experiences in some women's lives. Her sexual freedom, combined with a wardrobe that refused to objectify that freedom, resonated with both women who had never had that sort of relation to sex and women who were all too familiar with the additional labour that comes with such liberation. The focus in these interviews on Elaine's personal life rather than her working one suggests that these elements of her character stood out as being more pertinent to our mothers' own lives as well as their understandings of feminism. Although our mothers might have had complex relationships with feminism, they both modeled the importance of addressing gender-based inequalities for their daughters. Growing up watching Elaine as a figure of smart, capable, and hilarious womanhood in our lives surely shaped our understandings of what equality of the sexes and freedom of choice might look like and mean. Elaine Benes may not have been ultimately crowned queen of the castle, but she certainly was a master of her domain.

Endnotes

1. It should be noted that while Elaine is never explicitly identified as a feminist, there are numerous examples in which Elaine is aligned with mainstream feminism. In "The Couch," Elaine is disappointed to learn that her very "good-looking" date is antichoice. She highlights women's sexual needs and prioritizes her pleasure in "The Contest." And, finally, in (the dated and problematically titled) "The Handicap Spot," George makes a disparaging comment about "the feminists," and Elaine shoots him a dirty look and asks "What does that mean?"

2. Film theorist Laura Mulvey coined the term "male gaze" in her ground-breaking essay "Visual Pleasure and Narrative Cinema," which unpacks how the film viewer is positioned as an active male observer in contrast to the passive female subject who connotes "to-be-looked-at-ness." The positioning of male as active surveyor and female as an object of vision has a long history in Western visual culture, most notably explored in John Berger's history of European oil painting (1500–1900) through the Renaissance. Berger argues that this visual history works to create a different social presence for women—one based on performing for the male viewer and one of viewing themselves through a masculinist gaze.

3. Bonnie Dow notes that the titular strong female lead in *Murphy Brown* wore dark, bold colours in contrast to the pastel, flowing outfits worn by the more (traditionally) feminine Corky.

4. The correct quote from "The Shoes" is "put the asses in the seats."

Works Cited

Berger, John. *Ways of Seeing*. Vol. 1. Penguin UK, 2008.

Bettie, Julie. "Class Dismissed: *Rosanne* and the Changing Face of Working-Class Iconography." *Social Text*, vol. 45, winter, 1995, pp. 125-49.

Brook, Vincent. "From the Cozy to the Carceral: Trans-Formations of Ethnic Space in The Goldbergs and Seinfeld. (Critical Essay)." *Velvet Light Trap*, Sept., 1999, pp. 54.

Cooper, Evan. "I'm a Little Scared of' Elaine: Representations of Jewish and Gentile Women in *Seinfeld* and *Curb Your Enthusiasm*." *Studies in*

American Humour. 3.27 (2013): 93–115. Print.

David, Larry, and Jerry Seinfeld, creators. *Seinfeld.* Castle Rock Entertainment, 1989–1993.

Di Mattia, Joanna. "The Show About Something: Anxious Manhood and the Homosocial Order on *Seinfeld.*" *Michigan Feminist Studies,* vol. 14, 1999, pp. 59-81.

Dow, Bonnie J. "Hegemony, Feminist Criticism and the *Mary Tyler Moore* Show." *Critical Studies in Media Communication,* vol. 7, no. 3, 1990, pp. 261-74.

Faludi, Susan. *Backlash: The Undeclared War Against American Women.* Crown, 1991.

Grabowski, Michael. "Resignation and Positive Thinking in the Working-Class Family Sitcom." *Atlantic Journal of Communication,* vol. 22, no. 2, 2014, pp. 124-37.

Harrison, Kristen. "Does Interpersonal Attraction to Thin Media Personalities Promote Eating Disorders?" *Journal of Broadcasting & Electronic Media,* vol. 41, no. 4, 1997, pp. 478-500.

Hirsch, Irwin, and Cara Hirsch. "*Seinfeld*'s Humour Noir: A Look at Our Dark Side." *Journal of Popular Film and Television,* vol. 28, no. 3, 2000, pp. 116-23.

Kim, Janna L., et al. "From Sex to Sexuality: Exposing the Heterosexual Script on Primetime Network Television." *Journal of Sex Research,* vol. 44, no. 2, 2007, pp. 145-57.

Morreale, Joanne. "Sitcoms Say Goodbye: The Cultural Spectacle of *Seinfeld*'s Last Episode." *Critiquing the Sitcom: A Reader,* edited by Joanne Morreale, Syracuse University Press, 2003, pp. 274-85.

Mulvey, Laura. *Visual and Other Pleasures.* Palgrave Macmillan, 1989.

Pizam, Abraham. "Customer Saboteurs or 'Badvocates.'" *International Journal of Hospitality Management,* vol. 45, 2015, pp. 145-46.

Rabinovitz, Lauren. "Sitcoms and Single Moms: Representations of Feminism on American TV." *Cinema Journal,* vol. 29, no. 1, 1989, pp. 3-19.

Rowe, Kathleen. *The Unruly Woman : Gender and the Genres of Laughter.* University of Texas Press, 1995.

"Sexual Stereotypes Stop Females from Feeling Pleasure (Brief Article)." *SIECUS Report*, vol. 30, no. 4, 2002, p. 18.

Swink, Robyn Stacia. "Lemony Liz and Likable Leslie: Audience Understandings of Feminism, Comedy, and Gender in Women-Led Television Comedies." *Feminist Media Studies*, vol. 17, no. 1, 2017, pp. 14-28.

Chapter Nine

Lighten Up! Life as a Vegetarian Feminist, or the Most Uptight Person in the World

Margaret Betz

Humour, seriousness, and anger pose a tangled mess of conflicting cultural norms and expectations for women. On the one hand, culturally, we have reserved the description of "funny" primarily for men, and, on the other, we chastise women for taking things "too seriously," such as rape jokes, sexual come-ons, and enforced gender norms. As a self-identified feminist, I've had to tread carefully among these social landmines.

Eventually, I came to the realization that my life as a vegetarian involves similar social landmines and that, combined, these two chosen identities have earned me the reputation as all-around uptight. Since I stopped eating meat twenty-five years ago, I have noticed similarities between people's response to learning I'm a vegetarian and their response to learning I'm a feminist: unease and defensiveness. Rarely do I mention being a vegetarian, but when it does come up, I'm often met with responses that offer explanations of why meat is necessary to the speaker's diet, how the speaker doesn't eat that much meat, or just plain ridicule. To be sure, I wasn't the first to see a link between vegetarianism and feminism. Likely the most widely-known vegetarian feminist is Carol J. Adams, who wrote the book *The Sexual Politics of Meat* over thirty years ago. Adams argues that "A feminist's emphasis on sexual violence is judged as hysterical; a vegetarian's emphasis on the death of animals as emotional. Both feminists and vegetarians are accused of negativity because they appear to require that something be given up" (90). In my own life, humour is one way I have learned to navigate society's response to my chosen identities. My "Kale-Eating Feminist Killjoy" tee-shirt, for instance, manages to kill two birds with one stone.

Yet, apparently, the idea of women as funny still draws controversy. In 2013, American comedian Jerry Lewis announced at a Cannes Film Festival press conference that he was "bothered" watching female comedians. He explained, "I cannot sit and watch a *lady* diminish her qualities to the lowest common denominator" (my emphasis, "Jerry Lewis"). Lewis appears to juxtapose the idea of humour with what is proper feminine behaviour (i.e., ladylike). In addition to Lewis's implicit assumption that humour is monolithic, he critiqued women for allegedly debasing themselves by mimicking what's apparently the realm of men.

Lewis wasn't the first to assume that humour seems to be the domain of men. Cultural norms and standards have often demanded of women more restrained behaviour. Of course, there have always been funny women in everyday life, some of whom fought their way onto stages and screens and into print. Some have been decidedly indecorous too, like Ali Wong, Sarah Silverman, and Caitlin Moran. Although our culture is showing signs of changing, Lewis, nonetheless, vocalized a deeply ingrained collective belief: Being funny is not normally seen as the realm of women.

Six years before Lewis's comments, Christopher Hitchens published an article in *Vanity Fair* titled "Why Women Aren't Funny." Hitchens's piece is a combination of broad heteronormative brushstrokes, benevolent sexism, and condescension that assumes Lewis's understanding of what "funny" means. The general idea of Hitchens' essay is that because men have the role of pursuer in romantic interactions, they need humour as a tool to woo women. "The chief task in life that a man has to perform is that of impressing the opposite sex," Hitchens contends. Women, as passive recipients of romantic advances, have no such need because they are already attractive to men as is. Hitchens believes women can certainly appreciate humour but are not particularly skilled at being humorous themselves. He does admit however that impressive female comedians exist, but "most of them are ... hefty, dykey, or Jewish, or some combination of the three."

As with Lewis, Hitchens's polemic invites us to question what we even mean by "funny." He, too, assumes the same male-as-standard definition, saying "Male humour prefers to laugh at someone's expense." Because so much humour in commercial entertainment embodies this norm of humour at someone's expense, women who are not funny in this way are, therefore, often viewed as not funny at all. "Funny," as it turns out, is not only culturally prescribed but also gendered, too. Hitchens admits it is possible men don't want women to be funny, since that would create a rival. Men already stand in awe of women's ability to give birth, he claims, which gives women an "unchallenged authority." Both Lewis and Hitchens, then, admit to a male standard of what constitutes "funny" and their shared discomfort with the idea of women encroaching on this male space.

Likely referencing Hitchens's famous piece, feminist journalist Lindy West wrote a *New York Times* editorial called "Why Men Aren't Funny" in 2017, ten years after his original essay. In many ways a rebuttal to Hitchens, West's article addresses the #MeToo movement and the men accused, specifically the comedian Louis C.K. She quotes fellow comedian Marc Maron, who described his epiphany that women in the industry had to deal with sexual harassment and assault, unlike male comedians. Maron realized that female comedians "had to deal with us" to which West responds that women "have been pointing out [our] disadvantage in comedy for a very long time.... In return, we've been abused, discredited, blacklisted, turned into punchlines and driven out of the industry." West's point is there are reasons why there have been fewer high-profile female comedians over the years, comedians who may have widened the scope of what we think of as funny. She stresses that female comedians were deliberately and systematically kept down and pushed out of the industry.

Society is just as quick to characterize women as humourless, infamously embodied in the stereotype of the strident militant feminist (or "feminazi" as Rush Limbaugh calls them), who criticizes seemingly benign cultural norms and niceties. The "humourless feminist" trope isn't so much about whether or not she attempts to be funny but rather that she isn't receptive to the usual societal norms and expectations. A manifestation of the feminist-as-too-serious is the complaint that she can't take a joke. She makes everything a problem, which might have been the impetus behind *Vice* journalist Mitchell Sunderland asking alt-right provocateur Milo Yiannopoulos to mock Lindy West, to whom he referred as a "fat feminist." West, an admirably confident writer, pushes things too far, it would seem, beyond what is culturally expected of her as a woman and, particularly, as a large woman.

Feminist-as-humourless is often tied to identifying feminist-as-angry. Early feminist philosophers like Claudia Card, bell hooks, and Marilyn Frye wrote about the social perception of feminists as "feisty" and "angry," identifying these qualities as largely a refusal to accept the role of feminine passivity. These were the thinkers who helped shape my feminist sensibilities. It is no wonder second-wave feminism felt compelled to respond to characterizations of the humourless feminist; with the motto "the personal is political," feminist theorists of this generation sought to disrupt the socialization of the demure, compliant, and agreeable woman. Card writes of wanting to address topics that "violate rules of polite society [and] use vocabularies that transcend conventions of politeness" (17). She identifies "feistiness of insubordination" as a feminist virtue and praises the sustaining feistiness of feminist philosophers (18). Card believes that "humourless responses" by feminists show a "readiness to quarrel," reflecting a vitality that keeps the issues alive (18). In other words, the very qualities labelled so unappealing to the larger society are what give feminist theory its identity and motivation. Perhaps the desire to embrace the characterization of humourless by some second-wave feminists stemmed from an implicit belief at the time that women needed to first establish a cultural space for their anger.

In line with this, bell hooks writes of the significance of the phrase "talking back" to the southern Black community in which she grew up. Hooks identifies the home as the place Black women dominated with their speech, in contrast to the male-dominated churches, a place where hooks was inspired to find her own voice. She explains that the creation of her pseudonym "bell hooks" came after she had just spoken defiantly to an adult: "Even now I can recall the surprised look, the mocking tones, that informed me that I must be kin to bell hooks—a sharp tongued woman, a woman who spoke her mind, a woman who was not afraid to talk back. I claimed this legacy of defiance, of will, of courage, affirming my link to female ancestors who were bold and daring in their speech" (17).

Marilyn Frye tackles the topic directly in an essay titled "A Note on

Anger." The essay begins with the following statement: "It is a tiresome truth of women's experience that our anger is generally not well-received" (84). Frye attempts to distinguish just what we mean by "anger" and decides that it implies "a claim that one is a being whose purpose and activities require a web of objects, spaces, attitudes, and interests that is worthy of respect, and that the topic of this anger is a matter rightly within that web" (87). Women are often denied the right to assume being "worthy of respect," and Frye notes the response is often to call them "hysterical" or "crazy." That type of response, Frye argues, attempts to delegitimize the content of a woman's anger by refusing to engage with it. Instead, it opts for the well-worn cliché of female irrationality. If anger does indeed imply a "demand for respect" as Frye suggests, then there is no doubt why it can become a subversive tool for women. Frye ends the essay by surmising: "For better or for worse ... in each of our lives, others' concepts of us are revealed by the limits of the intelligibility of our anger" (93). Righteous anger tests the limits of respect. It's with these eyes that we can consider Sunderland's misogynist request of Yiannopoulos: the presumption that West deserved punishment for believing she had the right to her anger.

West discusses female anger in another *New York Times* article she wrote in the first weeks of the #MeToo movement, arguing that female anger is "weaponized against women," as it was against her. She notes that when women lose their temper in public, they often face a backlash. West arrives at a similar understanding as Frye, agreeing with her characterization that anger involves demanding that one's concerns are "worthy of respect." Women are expected to endure all sorts of hardships and forms of oppression, and as West argues, "we are not even allowed to be angry about it ... we are not expected to complain as we are diminished, degraded, and discredited." She adds: "I did not call myself a feminist until I was nearly twenty years old. My world taught me that feminists were ugly and ridiculous ... it took me two decades to become brave enough to be angry. Feminism is the collective manifestation of female anger. They suppress our anger for a reason. Let's prove them right."

Humour is indispensable to a lot of contemporary feminist writing and activism. Many feminists have combined their righteous anger with the use of humour, refusing to see them as opposing tactics. Jessica Valenti's *Full Frontal Feminism* is a good example. Written in a conversational style, this work is full of sarcasm and humour. For instance, when discussing the origin of engagement rings as signalling the woman now belongs to someone, Valenti adds, "So if men started wearing engagement rings, next thing you know, ear tags for women (maybe with their fiancé's income stamped on them) would become popular. I'm joking, but you get the point" (150).

Keeanga-Yamahtta Taylor's feminist commitments represent another example. Taylor interviewed important Black feminist activists for her book *How We Get Free*, including the major forces behind the 1977 Combahee River Collective Statement. Taylor writes that the collective recognized "oppression on the basis of identity—whether it be racial, gender, class, or sexual orientation identity—was a source of political radicalization" (8). Throughout, Taylor and her subjects maintain a humourous tone, which intermixes feminist theory, political activism, and biography. For instance, in an interview with Barbara Smith, addressing the racism Black feminists have faced from white feminists, Smith says, "The baloney, you know. 'I don't really see colour.' Well, time to go to the ophthalmologist" (50).

Nigerian author Chimamanda Ngozi Adichie uses both anger and humour in her book *Dear Ijeawele, or A Feminist Manifesto in Fifteen Suggestions*. Adichie sets out to compile a list of her best feminist advice for a childhood friend on how to raise her daughter as a feminist. Adichie writes: "Do you remember how we laughed and laughed at an atrociously written piece about me some years ago? The writer had accused me of being 'angry' as though 'being angry' were something to be ashamed of. Of course I am angry. I am angry about racism. I am angry about sexism" (22). Later in the book, Adichie considers the tradition of women taking their husbands' last name when they marry and muses:

> Mrs. can be a choice, but to infuse it with as much value as our culture does is disturbing. The value we give to Mrs. means the marriage changes the social status of a woman but not that of the man. (Is that perhaps why many women complain of married men still 'acting' as though they were single? Perhaps if our society asked married men to change their names and take on a new title, different from Mr., their behaviour might change as well? Ha!). (35)

Another contemporary writer who has perfected blending humour with feminism is British journalist Caitlin Moran. In an essay called "I am a Feminist," Moran writes:

> I realized that it's technically impossible for a woman to argue against feminism. Without feminism, you wouldn't be *allowed* to have a debate on a woman's place in society. You'd be too busy giving birth on the kitchen floor – biting down on a wooden spoon, so as to not disturb the men's card game – before going back to hoeing the rutabaga field…. The more women argue, loudly, against feminism, the more they both prove it exists and that they enjoy its hard won privileges. (my emphasis, 76)

In my own life, I've also used righteous anger and humour to prod and cajole. When I was as a college sophomore, my English professor— an older white priest—loved to use part of class time bantering with students about their clothes, hairstyles, and comments in class discussions. It often deteriorated into him essentially picking on his chosen target that day; eventually, it landed on me. I can't remember the specific content of his comments to me, but I pushed back. At the end of class, he assured me he was only joking, but I met his humour with my own. In response to his pronouncement that women only go to college to find husbands, I wrote him an anonymous letter telling him that although I didn't find a husband in my years at college, I did "find" being accepted into a philosophy master's program. I ended my letter by rhetorically questioning whether or not the university had an obligation to refund my tuition. I've always wondered what this priest was thinking when he read my letter, wondering which female student tested the limits by answering his jokes with her own feisty sarcasm.

Just as there exists a stereotype of the humourless feminist, the cultural face of veganism and vegetarianism hasn't fared much better. We are often depicted in memes and mainstream media as uptight, militant animal lovers, hellbent on converting or shaming you, or both. YouTube features over two thousand hits for pranking a vegetarian into eating meat. Both Gordon Ramsay and Anthony Bourdain have complained about vegans and vegetarians, the latter referring to vegetarians as "Hezbollah-like." It took some time for me to understand why these intolerant reactions towards feminists and ethical vegetarians were so similar: Both groups implicitly question the status quo and call upon cultures to change. Someone adopting a different norm, viewpoint, and way of living feels threatening to some. The YouTube vegetarian pranks and Sunderland's request to mock a "fat feminist" are examples of how those protecting the status quo look for ways to ridicule and undermine what makes them uncomfortable because of their attempts to change society.

Animal activist Mall Ball, the founder of One Step for Animals, argues that vegan and vegetarian animal advocates are partially to blame for their public perception by all-too-frequently contributing with harsh, berating messages that lack compassionate support and advice. In "How Vegans Hurt Animals," Ball wonders that if an intolerant approach didn't accompany a compelling argument, how much more successful vegan or vegetarian animal activism could be. He chastises fellow activists for insisting on "pushing a message we know people will automatically reject." Ball explains as follows:

> This is dead-simple obvious to anyone who has studied psychology or surveyed vegetarians. ("How many of you stopped eating meat because someone yelled 'GO VEGAN, you MURDERER!?' Anyone?") And yet for three decades I've been an advocate, there has *always* been a segment of vegans who have built vast and elaborate rationalizations for basing their "activism" on screaming and hatred (and attacking anyone who is not sufficiently pure and dogmatic).

Of course, Ball is right that any social movement can include people with a rigidity of vision. But how accurate is it to simply blame the self-righteousness of vegans or vegetarians for the public's perception of them? As it turns out, my instinct about the cultural threat vegetarians represent has been confirmed in moral psychology research. A study conducted in 2015 examined the public perception of vegans and vegetarians and found it overwhelmingly negative. Citing "vegophobia," researchers Cara MacInnis and Gordon Hodson present their findings in an article called, "It Ain't Easy Eating Green: Evidence of Bias toward Vegetarians and Vegans from Both Source and Target." They found that omnivores tend to judge vegans and vegetarians more harshly than other people with restricted diets (like those who maintain a gluten-free diet). Moreover, people who turn to veganism and vegetarianism for animal rights or environmental concerns were found to face the most bias. The researchers conclude the likely explanation is that these groups represent a symbolic threat to the status quo. Interestingly, those who register as holding the most negative beliefs against these groups were found to be people who align themselves with conservative political ideologies. MacInnis and Hodson determine this is likely due to the fact that these are the people most interested in conserving traditional lifestyles, and veganism and vegetarianism threaten to disrupt American meat-eating culture. This research theorizes that groups feel under attack if their implicit beliefs, values, and moral standards are challenged, and they feel others are threatening to undermine them.

There is a link to sexism here. First, MacInnis and Hodson also found that "male vegetarians and vegans were evaluated more negatively than female vegetarians and vegans respectively, and male (vs. female) omnivores evaluated vegetarian and vegan men more negatively, with this sex difference explained by *gender bias*" (my emphasis, 11). A common topic in animal rights literature is the role of meat in American society as symbolizing male dominance and superiority through, for example, hunting. To willingly forgo that superior status can be viewed by some as a suspicious self-feminization. Second, MacInnis and Hodson conclude that vegetarian and vegan values may be "viewed as undermining the current way of life, rendering vegetarian/vegans targets of negativity." Moreover, the authors stress that "Environmentalists and *feminists*, and other groups who do little objective harm but threaten the status quo are likewise evaluated by omnivores, presumably for similar reasons" (my emphasis, 19).

Reflecting on this research, I was reminded of Frye's identification of anger as "a claim that one is a being whose purpose and activities require a web of objects, spaces, attitudes, and interests that is worthy of respect, and that the topic of this anger is a matter rightly within that web." What I realized is the backlash against disrupting cultural norms doesn't even need to be in response to someone vocally challenging something. Simply by identifying as both a feminist and a vegetarian, I am symbolically demanding a level of respect for my concerns that will not always be well received, such as the time a man told me in a bar, "Don't wear striped stockings because someone might drop a house on you," when he became angry with our debate. Much research in moral psychology confirms what is known as the ingroup-outgroup phenomenon, when human beings are considering, often unconsciously, how to regard and treat people. As T.J. Kasperbauer describes in his book

Subhuman, we are constantly looking for markers to signify whether or not someone is a member of our ingroup or a member of an outgroup with which we don't identify. Members of an outgroup are often regarded with distrust. Feminists fit the description to the mainstream of an outgroup by threatening gender norms. So do vegetarians, for that matter, as do the animals themselves that vegetarians demand are worthy of respect. In this context, jokes about women and jokes about vegetarians may actually be examples of masked hostility towards the outgroup in question—a subtle attempt to deny that the individual and their concerns are worthy of respect, as was true for Lindy West.

Carol J. Adams offers an interesting interpretation of the significance of feminist vegetarianism. She writes that vegetarianism "reverberates with feminist meaning" because there's a link between the oppression of women and meat eating (13). According to Adams, "Vegetarianism [is] one way to reject a male world that [objectifies] both women and animals" (170). She argues that we render both women and animals commodities with "consumable bodies" so that vegetarianism "acts as a sign of autonomous female being and signals a rejection of male control and violence" (16).

Just as with my identification as a feminist, I've learned to use humour to deflect, poke, and cajole as a vegetarian, too. When a high school friend asked if I planned on attending a class reunion she described as a "pig roast," I responded, "Only if you don't mind me showing up with protest signs." In vegetarian writing and activism, however, humour is seen less frequently. Vegetarian writing tends to fall into two categories. The first is academic in nature and focuses on the moral questions surrounding humanity's attitudes and treatment of animals, and the second tends to aim at a more general audience and is best described as lifestyle oriented, offering advice on recipes, vegetarian-friendly eateries, and where to find vegan products. A combination of the two is animal activist organizations that offer the philosophy behind why people should make these lifestyle changes. None particularly lend themselves to approaching the topics of veganism and vegetarianism with humour. And because veganism and vegetarianism are lifestyles chosen for a host of reasons (for example, health, environmental, moral, and religious), not all of them equally involve a call to activism and social change. When humour does pop up in vegetarian writing and activism, it is mostly parenthetical, such as clever tee-shirts or sarcastic memes; rarely is it the central mechanism of the writing or activism itself.

Nevertheless, there are a couple of notable examples that use humour, one much like the type seen with feminist writers. Valenti, Adichie, and Moran all examine cultural norms we usually accept on face value and then exaggerate them to the point of absurdity. Humour here is used to shine light on our uncritical and often inconsistent thinking. Their purpose is not so much to accuse as it is an attempt to force us to consider why exactly do we think this way. Unlike Hitchens's description of (male) humour as "at someone's expense," this type of humour disarms by inviting the listener to laugh at our shared cultural absurdities and to imagine better possibilities.

An example of vegetarian activism that uses this type of humour is the work of the syndicated cartoonist Dan Piraro. The creator of the award-winning cartoon *Bizarro,* Piraro became interested in ethical vegetarianism through a girlfriend of his. He began using his daily newspaper cartoons as a way to satirize Americans' inconsistent attitudes towards animals, such as how they eat some animals and treat others like family members. Describing himself on his website as someone who stirs up controversy, Piraro's activism also takes the form of public lectures he calls "The Humourous Side of Vegetarianism." Videos of his speaking engagements are available on *YouTube.* In one, Piraro offers the usual host of topics, such as the health benefits of veganism, the awful conditions found in factory farms; the emotional and intellectual lives of animals, and the environmental impact of livestock. He jokes that he lost so much weight by becoming vegan that people in his home state of Oklahoma regard him as too thin and are "ready to stage an intervention." Piraro explains that the guiding principle of his veganism is that "it's up to me to be a less arrogant ape on this planet than I could be." In an interview, Piraro is asked if he sees it as his obligation to use his forum as a soapbox, to which he responds as follows: "Yes and no. I really feel like people's best work comes from what they feel and believe. I don't want to come off as preaching because I'm a new convert and have all the zeal. And I want to be clear: it's not about not eating meat. It's about not supporting an industry that abuses animals." Piraro delivers the same message as other animal activists but disarms his audience by not relying on a stereotypical preachy approach. As seen with the feminist writers, humour can be used as a means of establishing common ground. Piraro's announcement, for example, that he smokes cigars—"[because]

I got to have something to kill me off. I gotta have a vice"—draws laughter from his audience, with the implicit message that meat eating harms our health, but it also creates suffering for animals. If we are going to do things that kill us, we should find ways that don't kill animals, too.

Another example of humourous vegetarian writing is *Skinny Bitch*. Written in the same conversational style as Valenti's *Full Frontal Feminism*, Rory Freedman and Kim Barnouin combine their ethical- and health-based veganism and humour. The book promises to deliver not a "diet" but a "way of life," which will allow readers to enjoy food, feel healthy and energized, and become skinny. They warn about the hostility against vegetarians and vegans by advising the following: "Keep your eyes peeled for bad press regarding veganism. It's usually planted by the industries that are threatened by the movement. Don't believe any of it" (182). Though clever, irreverent, and informative, Freedman and Barnouin inaccurately equate a plant-based diet with being skinny, ignoring the reality that body shape and size are not reducible to just food choices. They use such cringe-worthy phrases as "Don't be a fat pig anymore" and suggest women have "lumpy ass[es]" because of the harmful effects of aspartame in diet sodas. The authors also criticize people who balk at spending the extra money for healthier organic produce as being "cheap asshole[s]," overlooking the fact that fresh fruits and vegetables are already a luxury for people living in economically vulnerable neighbourhoods without supermarkets. Anticipating Matt Ball's complaint, Freedman and Barnouin end the book by advising: "Spread the good word, but be careful not to preach. You'll see that some people get very defensive about their diets when you tell them about yours. Even if you're being very non-judgmental, people will feel threatened by your righteousness. But never ... make them feel bad about their diet" (186-87).

Skinny Bitch serves a cautionary tale about the dangers of myopic vision: Dedication to social change in one area doesn't justify reinforcing damaging cultural stereotypes and norms in other areas. Even if it is tongue in cheek, Freedman and Barnouin rely throughout on sexist standards, fat shaming, and class-based assumptions, which follow Hitchens's "humour at someone's expense" model. The authors claim to be motivated by empowering women, but it ends up applying only to a particular segment of women. Just like Barbara Smith's complaint to Keeanga-Yamahtta Taylor about white feminists' racism towards Black feminists, social activism ultimately falls flat if it reinforces prejudice and marginalization in other areas. Smith and Adams are both excellent examples of intersectional feminists committed to recognizing and addressing how systems of power and oppression intersect.

It is my aim for my vegetarian feminism to honour the insights of intersectional feminism. Both of these characterizations will continue to represent a perceived threat to norms that some don't want to see change. Based on these chosen identities, I may be perceived as humourless and uptight—that I take seemingly inconsequential things too seriously. Part of choosing identities that are disruptive means to accept being on the figurative frontlines of the battle and fighting the good fight with confidence and humour. As Caitlin Moran says about the next wave of feminism: "I would hope that the main thing that distinguishes it from all that came before it is that women counter the awkwardness, disconnect, and bullshit of being a modern woman not by shouting at it, internalizing it, or squabbling about it—but by simply pointing at it and going 'HA!' instead" (14). Frye may say it is a "tiresome truth" that this path is not easy. Yet to quote West: "They suppress our anger for a reason. Let's prove them right." And the best part? I'm funny, too. Just ask my English professor.

Works Cited

Adams, Carol J. *The Sexual Politics of Meat: A Feminist-Vegetarian Critical Theory*. Continuum, 1990.

Adichie, Chimamanda Ngozi. *Dear Ijeawele, or a Feminist Manifesto in Fifteen Suggestions*. Alfred A. Knopf, 2017.

Ball, Matt. "How Vegans Hurt Animals." *One Step for Animals*, 2018, www.onestepforanimals.org/. Accessed 29 Dec. 2020.

Card, Claudia. "The Feistiness of Feminism." *Feminist Ethics*, edited by Claudia Card, University of Kansas, 1991, pp. 3-31.

Freedman, Rory and Barnouin, Kim. *Skinny Bitch*. Running Press, 2005.

Frye, Marilyn. "A Note on Anger." *Politics of Reality: Essays in Feminist Theory*. Crossing Press, 1983, pp. 84-94.

Heintjes, Tom. "Mondo Bizzaro: The Dan Piraro Interview." *Cartoonician*, 25. Dec. 2017, cartoonician.com/mondo-bizarro-the-dan-piraro-interview/. Accessed 29 Dec. 2020.

Hitchens, Christopher. "Why Women Aren't Funny." *Vanity Fair*, 1 Jan. 2007, www.vanityfair.com/culture/2007/01/hitchens200701. Accessed 29 Dec. 2020.

Hooks, bell. "Talking Back." *Women: Images and Realities*, 5th edition, edited by Suzanne Kelly, Gowri Parameswaran, and Nancy Schniedewind, McGraw Hill, 2012, pp. 15-18.

"Jerry Lewis: 'Women Doing Comedy Bothers Me." Independent, 24 May 2013, www.independent.co.uk/arts-entertainment/films/news/jerry-lewis-women-doing-comedy-bothers-me-8630459. html. Accessed 12 Jan. 2021.

Kasperbauer, T.J. *Subhuman: The Moral Psychology of Human Attitudes to Animals*. Oxford, 2018.

MacInnis, Cara, and Gordon Hodson. "It Ain't Easy Eating Greens: Evidence of Bias towards Vegetarians and Vegans from Both Source and Target." *Group Process & Intergroup Relations*, vol. 20, 2015, pp. 1-24.

Moran, Caitlin. *How to Be a Woman*. Harper, 2011.

Piraro, Dan. "The Humourous Side of Vegetarianism." *YouTube*, 10 Jan. 2009, www.youtube.com/watch?v=IPfFjEmMgkU. Accessed 29 Dec. 2020.

Taylor, Keeanga-Yamahtta. *How We Get Free: Black Feminism and the Combahee River Collective*. Haymarket Books, 2017.

Valenti, Jessica. *Full Frontal Feminism: A Young Woman's Guide to Why Feminism Matters*. 2nd ed. Seal Press, 2014.

West, Lindy. "Brave Enough to Be Angry." *The New York Times*, 8 Nov. 2017, www.nytimes.com/2017/11/08/opinion/anger-women-weinstein-assault.html. Accessed 29 Dec. 2020.

West, Lindy. "Why Men Aren't Funny." *The New York Times*, 14 Nov. 2017, www.nytimes.com/2017/11/14/opinion/louis-ck-not-funny-harassment.html. Accessed 29 Dec. 2020.

Chapter Ten

That Time I Tried to Date a Frat Boy

Alyson Rogers

As a straight-A feminist nerd who spent her undergrad days chasing men's rights activists off campus, I know I'm an unlikely expert on the frat boy community. To be honest, by the time I graduated, I had never even met a frat boy, let alone received an invitation to one of their parties. This, however, never stopped me from mocking them—I'm a feminist, mocking clueless cis/het boys is basically my birthright. Despite this heritage, I ended up in a brief but intense situationship with a member of a local Greek institution. Rather than bury what I witnessed during that dark time deep in my psyche, I am choosing to share my hard-earned knowledge here with you. Before dating a frat boy, there are some warnings you should heed about their traditions, culture, customs, and practices.

The fraternity house stood out on its street. It was an historical building in the heart of a city that values the new. The house was stately and beautiful. Then I stepped inside. There is no nice way to put this (but I'm not writing this to be nice), so I will just say it—that house was nasty. It was so filthy that even the frat boys themselves refused to use their own kitchen. They blamed it on the season: "Oh, it's summer, so we haven't cleaned yet." It didn't look like they cleaned in the fall, winter, or spring either. If you ever meet me in person, don't worry, my shots are up to date and I never slept there.

The kitchen, while disgusting, was at least obviously so. Other areas of the house were no more likely to pass a health inspection, but they hid their grime well enough that you might be lulled into touching a surface with your bare skin. Not that frat houses are known for being safe spaces, but there wasn't even a safe space to sit. There are no safe places to sit because generations of frat boys' sweaty bare asses have been grinding on every couch they own. Having sex on the couches is practically a frat boy rite of passage. Forget being blood brothers, these bros carry their legacy in dried butt sweat applied via pleather. My advice? BYO HazMat suit or sit at your own risk.

The public health advisory on sitting applies to the frat house bathroom as well. Should you survive long enough within the house to need to relieve yourself, the hover method is your best bet. Thanks to the toilet that had never even heard rumour of a Lysol wipe, I've got thighs of steel and perfect aim. Despite the curious articles that frat houses tend to collect, what with so many people passing through them, the one I frequented had a chronic shortage of hand towels and soap. With that being said, shake a frat boy's hand at your own risk. The one time I saw a hand towel and soap I thought it was so nice that one of the frat boys was finally taking pride in his home and hand hygiene. With a second glance and sinking feeling, I noticed the soap and hand towel matched.

My immediate thought was "There is a woman in this house." There is a woman here, and I need to find her. Is she here willingly? Is the matching hand towel and soap actually a sign? A cry for help that only I could understand? I found her safe and sound; she was a courageous subletter, and she deserves an award for playing Florence Nightingale to a troupe of willfully grubby frat boys-cum-negligent landlords. So many questions lingered between us, the biggest being why sublet here of all places? The answer was cheap rent. Frat policy allowed spare rooms to be rented to women during the summer. Was this a new equity initiative to address women's struggle to find affordable housing? Probably not. Big city housing markets have gotten so bad in terms of high rents that women are subletting from frat houses for their summer internships. Would you live in a frat house if you only had to pay $750 per month for rent? Find out tonight on the next episode of *Fear Factor*.

This is where I wish this story would have ended. I could have seen the disarray and walked out the door, or I could have given you the ending you're not-so-secretly hoping for—that I set that frat house on fire. To our collective disappointment, this chapter is still titled "That Time I Tried to Date a Frat Boy," not "Honey, I Blew Up the Frat House."

I had my reservations about dating a frat boy and spending time at his home. I'd seen the kitchen, and I'd seen the bathroom. I knew what I knew about the couches and vowed to never sleep over. I'm a feminist who works in social services and is passionate about social justice. I know better than to touch a frat boy with a ten foot pole. But if the woman with the matching hand towels and soap could live with them, I figured that I could certainly handle dating one of them.

Despite their self-defined reputations as "ladies' men," the frat boys I knew offered virtually no accommodations to the women in their lives. A "Saturdays are for the Boys" sign has become the latest trend in bro home décor, and it was the centrepiece of their house. When you enter, the sign will be pointed out to you as a prized possession and, in my opinion, as a naked threat. When Saturdays are for the boys, you'll meet a frat boy's friends early on and often in your relationship.

Frat boys are an awkward bunch when you first meet them. They all want to know how you're connected to the frat, which allows them to evaluate how sexually available you may be to them. I wouldn't be surprised if there was a family tree-style hookup map on a whiteboard hidden somewhere in that house to document this information. It's important to keep track of these things. #BroCode.

After being grilled about your connection to the frat house, it's fun to turn this line of questioning back onto them. How are they connected to the frat? They get very defensive. How do they know your frat boy? They're brothers, of course! How else would they know them? What a silly question. It's not as if any other people or life exists outside the frat house walls. I still wonder if any of those guys are actually related. Everyone is their "brother for life," so I guess we'll never know.

The frat boys' summer house is whatever bar is a) nearest and b) stocked with plenty of chairs, with zero expectations to dance. It is an unwritten requirement that a frat boy be blackout drunk if they plan to leave the house after sundown—a perverted version of vampirism. I would often arrive at the bar to see all of his friends carousing without my particular boy in sight. Even though my frat boy was MID (missing in drunkness), the #BroCode remained strong. This gave me the extremely rare experience of sitting among the frat boys without having to worry about them hitting on me.

I took this opportunity of close proximity without fear of having my ass grabbed to make the world a better place. By make the world a better place, I mean furthering my feminist agenda. I became Wendy to the Lost Boys and, oh, were they lost. I taught valuable life lessons, such as you don't have to physically touch a woman in order to talk to her. I also put the law degree I don't have to good use to explain age of consent laws, which is some handy information to have in your back pocket when you're in your mid-twenties and still living in a frat house. Cancel Frosh Week and just set me up with a PowerPoint presentation in their main room; the weird skull paddles and pictures of old white men on the walls will provide enough ambiance, but bring your own chairs.

The frat boys were generous with me. They were happy to share their encyclopedic knowledge of drinking games, mixology, and rituals associated with different shots of alcohol. In return I'd hoist my Party Girl hat right over my Feminist Killjoy cap and share some knowledge of my own. Most notably, we never, under any circumstances, leave the dance floor during "Dancing Queen"—an empty drink is no excuse; it just means you have more freedom to groove.

I also tried to make changes to the state of their home. One day, my frat boy mentioned that the frat house was getting a new couch. I was ecstatic. There was no one more excited about that couch than I was. We spent most of our time together at my apartment for obvious sanitation reasons, so my frat boy was confused at my excitement. I'm into home décor, but this was a bit much. He didn't understand that this was my moment. This was my opportunity to ensure that one couch in their entire house remained untouched, unstained, and a safe place for me to sit.

We needed to move fast. That couch needed to be roped off, Scotchguarded or covered in plastic like an Italian grandmother's living room set. As I was working out a plan in my head, this boy went and broke my heart by telling me the couch had arrived the day before. Knowing the frat boys, they'd likely launched a contest to christen it. A moment of silence for the safe butt space that almost was.

I became a semisympathetic ear to the frat boys and provided sound (and obvious) advice to the myriad dating mysteries they encountered. The last three women you approached turned you down? Maybe you should keep your hands to yourself with the next one and see what happens. Success! The girl you really like doesn't like your friends? Take her somewhere that isn't the frat house. Your girlfriend is annoyed that you're drunk all the time? Time to test and see if you'll actually die if you leave the house sober after sundown. Your frat culture is getting in the way of you having a meaningful and fulfilling relationship? Grow up and move out. I'm a genius at giving dating advice. This is how I use my expensive piece of paper that says I finished a social work degree.

My frat boy and I eventually stopped seeing each other. A feminist and a frat boy, it would have never worked out. This left the question of what would happen to the frat boy's friends and me. Was the #BroCode strong enough that they would bar me from the house? The odds were stacked against me: I was a feminist who gave life lessons critical of their entire culture, and now one of their brothers for life was locked in his room crying to "Dancing Queen" on repeat and swearing never to go back to the bars I frequented. Despite all of this, they let me back in! More than once! I was a killjoy whom one of their brothers was avoiding like the plague and who wasn't putting out for anyone, and they still let me in. Either their screening process has gotten sloppy, or sometime between beer pong and foosball, this crew of frat boys decided my big ol' feminist heart and mind might be worth more than my booty.

So, what is the moral of this story? Is there some deeper meaning here? Should feminists start dating frat boys? Did I fix them? Should you start swiping right to all of the frat boys on Tinder and Bumble? Should you bang down the door of your local frat house and join their party? I've got my doubts. If, for whatever reason, you do find yourself in their midst don't hesitate to give me a shout. I've still got a stockpile of bleach and a Women's Studies for Frat Boys syllabus I'm more than happy to share.

Discussion questions:

1. What, if any, assumptions does this piece make about gender? Does it also trouble these assumptions and, if so, how?
2. Rogers writes, "There is no nice way to put this (but I'm not writing this to be nice), so I will just say it." Put this piece in conversation with Anitra Goriss-Hunter's and Sai Amulya Komarraju's chapters on unruly, modern women. How do gendered expectations of niceness and politeness influence how women's humour is received? How does this change based on who the audience is?
3. Media created by women is often scrutinized using the question, is this feminist? How does this all-or-nothing approach affect how we

analyze this content? What other questions could we be asking? Using Hayley R. Crooks and Stephanie Patrick's chapter as a launching point, consider what methodologies could be used to conduct a nuanced analysis of Rogers's piece.

4. Write a reflexive analysis on your experience of reading this piece. Which jokes were successful for you? Where did you smile or laugh? Which jokes made you groan or provoked no response from you at all? Do you notice any thematic similarities across these lists? Although people often claim that looking too closely at humour will kill the joke, what can we gain by practicing conscious and critical readings of comedy?

Notes on Contributors

Aba Amuquandoh is an actress, writer, and recent graduate of the University of Toronto with a major in drama. Aba is a playwright, a director, and she also teaches from time to time. Her most recent plays include *I Can't Trust Anyone, Everyone Hurts Me: A Comedy,* and *Ghanada.*

Margaret Betz is a philosophy professor at Rutgers University—Camden. She is the author of various articles and the book *The Hidden Philosophy of Hannah Arendt.* Margaret's love of animals and her sense of humour coalesced in naming her companion animals after mythical Greek figures, resulting in Greek comedies everyday.

Natalja Chestopalova is a writer and senior researcher at the Centre for Indigenous Visual Culture at OCAD University in Toronto. Her work is informed by the study of phenomenology, archival aesthetics, and psychoanalysis, and focuses on the transformative sensory experience and multimodality in film, the graphic novel medium, and theatrical site-specific performances.

Hayley R. Crooks employs youth participatory methodologies and video to examine gendered tech-facilitated violence with young people. Dr. Crooks uses her expertise to create participatory approaches to foster youth engagement in research (most recently with the *www. equalityproject.ca*) and has published in anthologies, peer-reviewed journals, and web-based magazines.

Marley Duckett is a master's candidate in environmental anthropology at the University of Saskatchewan. Her research focuses on relationships Indigenous Peoples have with resource extraction on treaty land in Canada. She is also passionate about artistic performance, particularly about how marginalized women use comedy to articulate social stresses impacting their lives.

Anna Frey is a sexual health and abortion counsellor, dedicated volunteer, and dog-parent to an unruly poodle. Anna lives and works in Toronto.

Anitra Goriss-Hunter is a lecturer in the School of Education at Federation University. Her teaching and research fields are in the following areas: gender and education, inclusion, and preservice teacher education. In 2011, Anitra was awarded the prestigious Australian Women's and Gender Studies PhD Award for the most outstanding thesis.

Sai Amulya Komarraju is a doctoral researcher in the Department of Communication, University of Hyderabad. Her research interests include feminist media studies, feminist cultural studies, and digital culture. Her doctoral research explores how Indian millennials understand gender, gender politics, feminisms, and feminist parenting in India. In her free time, she follows YouTube fan wars and DIY culture.

Stephanie Patrick obtained her PhD from the University of Ottawa in 2019. Her work examines the political economy of female celebrity and sexual violence in the media. Other research interests include sitcoms, reality television, news analysis, feminist theory, and social media.

Alyson Rogers is a mental health counsellor for children and youth at a health centre. She has a degree in Social Work from Ryerson University and is a registered yoga teacher. Alyson resides in St. Catharines, ON.

Vanessa Voss is a philosophy professor at Lone Star College. She focuses mainly on humour, as well as feminist and comparative philosophy. She is working on a larger project analyzing the concept of God through the lens of humor. Vanessa can often be found seeking what passes as happiness at dog parks.

Deepest appreciation to
Demeter's monthly Donors

DEMETER

Daughters
Rebecca Bromwich
Summer Cunningham
Tatjana Takseva
Debbie Byrd
Fionna Green
Tanya Cassidy
Vicki Noble
Bridget Boland
Naomi McPherson
Myrel Chernick

Sisters
Kirsten Goa
Amber Kinser
Nicole Willey
Christine Peets